Praise for How

In her book *How Goc*   ..., Susan shows her amazing story of God's power to restore the broken, redeem the lost, and reconcile those who are away from Him. Your heart will be encouraged as you read her story and discover the fact that, "with God, all things are possible."

> — Dr. David Cooper
> Senior Pastor
> Mount Paran Church of God

A book like this does not come along very often, which makes it a must read. Susan's story about her life is unbelievable. How anyone can live through this amount of spiritual turmoil is amazing. On the bright side the grace of God prevails, and His love brings peace and fulfillment to her life. It's a message to all of us: never give up as God is always with us and all we have to do is seek his loving guidance.

> — Carl Landwehr
> Founder
> Vitae Foundation

Susan Jaramillo's life story is compelling, her words are captivating, and this book is transformational. That is because her daily life is an ongoing work of God encounters and courageous conversations. I have seen the fruit of her life as a doctoral student and a life coach, and you will bear fruit from this read. There is hope here and help now for you to become fully awake to how God is rewriting your heart.

> — Dr. Joseph Umidi
> Professor of Practical Ministry
> Regent University School of Divinity

Susan is clear, forthright, and unsparing in her self-evaluation while lavishly thanking God and her prayerful mentors for their transforming intervention. I recommend this book to anyone wrestling with the brokenness of being human in a fallen world. If you are ready for freedom or desire to help others finally overcome their besetting issues, read this story and experience grace.

> — Dr. Charlie Self
> Professor of Church History
> Assemblies of God Theological Seminary

After many years of struggle, Susan finally discovered the only One that can deliver us from the spirits of addiction, abortion, and witchcraft. The One who gave His life so we can be free. Whether you consider them sin or disease, there are no worldly cures. But, there is One not of this earth who forgives, heals us, and can keep us free. That One is our Lord and Savior Jesus Christ. Susan's struggles are a testimony to the cure. I pray that her testimony will be encouragement for those who read this book.

> — Rev. John M. Franich, MDiv.
> Pastoral Counselor
> Founder & President
> Shenandoah Valley Teen Challenge

When I heard Susan's testimony in the Regent University Chapel, I was amazed at how God's grace can rescue anyone from the very depths of sin and despair. *How God Rewrote My Heart* is a stirring story of salvation and redemption. I highly recommend this book to anyone who needs a deep redeeming touch from God.

> — Dr. Vinson Synan
> Dean Emeritus
> Regent University School of Divinity

Mark Twain said, "The two most important days in your life are the day you are born and the day you find out why." Susan Jaramillo has definitely discovered why she was put on this earth, and that discovery came through her willingness to journey through the pain and losses she's experienced to enter into God's grace. I have witnessed true humility in Susan as she allows God's Word to transform her. Her passion to follow God's lead to share this journey— from captivity to freedom, from brokenness to wholeness, from following her will to surrendering to His will—is truly inspiring.

> — Lori Driggs
> Founder & Executive Director
> If Not for Grace Ministries

How God Rewrote My Heart is a testimony to a Redeemer God who "abundantly pardons and saves to the uttermost." Susan Jaramillo's story chronicles a personal journey lived under the assumption that she could navigate life by her own rules: without the God factor. Fortunately God rescued her from the consequences of poor decisions and self-destructive behavior. Susan's life was deeply transformed, and she is now a living testimony to the fact that God still intersects our lives with hope, peace, and grace that is more than sufficient. Reading this book will not only provide a narrative that many people may identify with, but a significant challenge that—when the "old passes away" and the "new comes"—the changes are those that only God could have provided.

> — Dr. Byron D. Klaus
> President
> Assemblies of God Theological Seminary

How God
rewrote my heart

How God
rewrote my heart

SUSAN JARAMILLO

HIGH BRIDGE BOOKS
HOUSTON

High Bridge Books
www.HighBridgeBooks.com

Printed in the United States of America
ISBN 978-1-940024-29-5

Book cover design: Firehouse Design
Photo by: Jill Bruss Photography
Special Thanks: Tim Morris

"'For I know the plans I have for you,' declares the LORD, 'plans to prosper you and not to harm you, plans to give you a hope and a future.'"
— Jeremiah 29:11

CONTENTS

With love and gratitude
to my mother and my children

PROLOGUE

It is my honor to write this forward for my friend Susan Jaramillo's new book, *How God Rewrote My Heart*.

When you are speaking before an audience, you usually do not know the people, their personal problems, or the particulars of their past; you just sense that somehow your message is going to spill out into their lives and hopefully make a difference. This is how I met Susan Jaramillo at a Junior League meeting. I was the keynote speaker that night. There she was—a beautiful, blonde, divorced mother of two. She fit my mentoring specialty—a single mother! Susan came forward after the talk and asked if we could get together for lunch. We did. That is how our friendship began.

Smart, attractive, and confident, Susan Jaramillo is a woman on a mission. I compared her to a fine thoroughbred racehorse biting at the bit to charge out of the stall to go for the prize. My first thought was to slow her down and to get her on a solid biblical foundation, if possible. I could see that Susan needed to be aware that hurrying can lead to making wrong choices. I enlisted the help of my friend Amy, a seasoned mentor and well-respected Christian leader. The two of us tag-teamed our new charge.

As Susan began to tell her life story, I saw caution signs that seasoned mentors recognize. Her story was profound. She talked. I listened. She cried. I prayed. Susan spilled out her sins, sorrows, and sad story. I listened and prayed more. What came from these mentoring times was phenomenal. Susan began to emerge stronger and willing to be mentored. She began to personally study the Bible, and to attend women's Bible classes and conferences. While still in the midst of custody battles, financial disasters, and strong opposition to uncovering dark family secrets, she discovered that there was a rich spiritual life available. Her new walk would require patience and perseverance. God was making Susan new.

With loss after loss, Susan's journey ultimately led her back to her hometown in Missouri. But again, this was God's plan. Often, God takes us back to our roots or our beginnings to remake us. *How God Rewrote My Heart* is Susan's powerful story of unlocking secrets, facing her past, and ultimately finding final emotional healing.

In *How God Rewrote My Heart*, Susan shares her rich life experiences. She gives God the glory for her turn-around and declares that the reader will walk away encouraged and more prepared to deal with life's hard issues. Susan credits God for rewriting a life of hurt and loss into a glorious life of trust, hope, and a new heart!

Susan's enthusiasm for her God-assignments are spilled out all over the pages of her book. Frank and transparent, she pours out her life's story. By all means read this book and pass it on to a friend.

Ann Platz
Author, Speaker, Designer
Atlanta, Georgia

ONE

TIRED OF HIDING BEHIND A MASK

"Create in me a pure heart, O God,
and renew a steadfast spirit within me.
Do not cast me from your presence
or take your Holy Spirit from me.
Restore to me the joy of your salvation
and grant me a willing spirit, to sustain me."
— Psalm 51:10-12

January 2007. It seemed I had no place to turn. I wanted my life to change, but didn't know how to change it. I tried to stop the addictions. While pretending on the outside that I had it together, my world was falling apart.

Keeping up the appearance of having it all together can wear on a person. Having played tough for 35 years, I was accustomed to relying on myself—

financially, emotionally, mentally, and spiritually. *Trust* did not exist in my vocabulary; it seemed everyone was out to get me. Life was an uphill climb.

* * *

December 2006. I prayed my life would change. When I say *pray*, I use the term loosely. I was brought up in church, but prayer usually meant I was asking for something I wanted.

When the women at my church organized a women's mentoring conference, I decided to attend. This event would take place one night a week over the next few months, and national speaker and author Ann Platz would focus on "Mentoring, a Spiritual Blessing of Grace."

I had met Ann in January of 2006 at an event sponsored by Junior League, an educational and charitable women's organization. She was a Southern belle who had it all together. She was strong, confident, and polished; she dressed, looked, and spoke the part. Instantly I respected her. But there was something I couldn't pinpoint—a presence that made her different. While listening to her that first time at Junior League, I felt my heart tugging, insisting I talk with her. When she finished speaking, I got up and met her at the back of the room and asked if I could take her to lunch.

Within weeks we met for lunch at her favorite place, the OK Cafe in the Buckhead district of Atlanta. She spoke about the HGTV show she had done, *Cullisaja Southern Living Christmas House 1998*. With a background in interior design, I had just done a pilot for a TV design show. We met a few times at her lovely home to discuss possibilities of doing a TV show together. I thought, *Surely, this is it! This is the timing and the ticket for my future. God, You better show up. I want a TV show with her to come through.* The ideas didn't flow. The quest to do a show together faded.

* * *

Having met that previous January, we were together again a year later. I felt guilty when I arrived for the mentoring conference. I had met a friend for dinner at Marietta Square earlier that evening, and we strolled in late—something I knew was unacceptable to Ann. I immediately became captured by the words Ann spoke.

"Where Satan has hit you hardest," she said, "that is your area of ministry."

Wow, I thought. *How will He ever use me?*

"Stop gossiping, and start encouraging," she continued. "Stop complaining, and start praying. Stop worrying, and be a person of faith. You conquer fear by having more faith."

I thought, *Where do you get faith?*

Ann said, "To know the Word of God, you have to study the Bible. To become a woman of prayer, you must give your fears to Him."

Although fear was an area I lived under, I didn't recognize it as fear until she talked about it.

"You must come under the authority of God and those whom He places over you," Ann said. "This includes your pastors, your husband, mentors, and others."

I thought, *Falling under authority is not something I do well.*

She continued, "Develop a life of spiritual discipline and integrity. You must walk the walk."

My reaction was, *OK, and how am I going to do that? I have too many secrets I've hidden behind closed doors.*

She added, "Open your heart to give and receive forgiveness."

I thought, *What? Receive forgiveness? How am I going to receive anything? There's no way. Forgive all those who've hurt me? Say I'm sorry?* My heart had become so hardened from the years of pain, hardship, and disappointments with others and with myself.

Last she said, "Trust God in every area of your life. This includes your hopes and dreams."

I couldn't believe it. It was as if no one else was in the room and she was speaking directly to me. She identified every area where I was struggling. She challenged me to look at myself, and I didn't want to. At the same time, I wanted to.

Ann explained what mentoring was. She brought two guest speakers, Amy and Jewell. Amy spoke about recognizing one as a mentee. Jewell spoke about what a healthy relationship looked like and how she felt called to wait on God for a mate. I was drawn to things that were missing from my life: forgiveness, healing, a deep walk with God, the ability to hear God's voice, and grace—**G**od's **R**elational **A**cceptance that **C**overs **E**verything. I thought, *Who is this God they are referring to? I don't know this God. The God I know is condemning, full of rules and restrictions, and way above me in the hierarchy. Who is this God who loves me unconditionally and wants to have a personal relationship with me? What is this healing He does?*

As Ann spoke that evening, she had such a sense of joy that encapsulated her. At times it was a little much for me, but I still recognized she had something I wanted. Her presence permeated the room, and her speech seemed to offer a secret for each woman who attended.

I was drawn into the conference, but the time was nearing 9 p.m. I was not happy. I would soon be missing my Thursday night TV show. I was ready to be home, popping open a beer, sitting in front of the fireplace, and watching my show, knowing my children were at their father's for the night.

Ann called us up front and asked us to get with someone we didn't know. I partnered with someone. She then asked us to be quiet and ask God to tell us a word that would speak to this person's heart. My thought was, *Are you kidding?* but shifted quickly to, *Where am I going to get this word? God, if You exist, You'd better give me a word so I don't look like a fool.* I was about to be exposed. Then I received this word. I had no idea if this was real or not. I spoke this word to the woman. She began to cry. I couldn't believe it! I was excited! I was also relieved I wasn't found out to be a fake and no one knew I wasn't living this life they had been speaking about.

Then Ann asked us to get into groups of three. My friend Debbie from church was right there. Although she did not know my inner struggles and torments, I found comfort in her and went to her group. Amy joined us.

While Ann prayed over the group, Amy stood between us and laid a hand on each of our shoulders. Amy's hand laid at the center of my back, I felt this jolt of energy, a sensation I had never felt before. When Ann was finished, I looked at Deb and asked, "Did you feel that?" Amy smiled. I had a word for my partner, and now I was feeling energy on my back where Amy's hand touched me.

At home, I popped open a beer, lit a cigarette, and sat down to blow the smoke out of the chimney. Tonight, something wasn't right. My beer didn't taste good. My cigarette wasn't the same. I threw them away. I asked myself, *How can this be, something that I've done for so many years?* I did not watch the rest of the TV show that night and never watched it again.

My heart tugged again over the next few days with a deep desire for healing and change, leading me to send Ann the following e-mail:

> January 24, 2007
> Hello Ann,
>
> I would like your wisdom and guidance on a few things.
>
> I always feel the presence of the Lord any time you're involved, and last week was no different. Amy put her hand on me, and it was

like a jolt of energy. That is the best way I can describe it; how amazing. I told her that.

I need to heal from all the wounds I've experienced: not knowing who my dad is (my mother will not tell me), losing our house and all of the struggles that went along with that time in high school, a failed marriage, etc. An awful amount of hatred lingers inside and shows its colors when I'm pushed too far.

Ann, I want my soul rejuvenated in Christ's love and filled with joy where all I feel is love. How do I get there? How does this awful feeling deep down inside escape from me? As I write with tears rolling down my face, I have feelings of disappointment and shame.

My mouth can be my worst enemy, and I have recognized this from a young age. Those who really know me only see this side since I've become so good at hiding behind the smile. I notice my son Tyler with some of this as well, and feel his pain of watching his mother and father fight as he was too young to understand all that was going on.

Thank you again for all you do for the good of the Lord. You are truly a blessing in my life that I cannot ignore. I knew it from the first word that came from your mouth. I love you, Ann, and I need your help to get me on the road to become a true woman of God and servant to others.

> Love you,
> Susan

Ann instructed me to call Amy, the one who had laid her hand on my back the previous week. Once Amy and I connected, we met that next week at Garrison's, one of Amy's favorite restaurants.

When we began visiting over lunch, I poured out my soul to a complete stranger. I had never shared so much, including my childhood, my past relationships, and my failed marriage, up to the present day. Somehow I let my guard down. Was I ready to surrender what had held me captive for so many years? The list was endless: rejection, hurt, pain, disappointment, lack of love, hatred for myself and others, anger, bitterness, resentment, brokenness, abandonment, loneliness, sadness, depression, and the lies. And the alcohol, drugs, and hurtful relationships. Two hours flew by.

Leaving the restaurant, Amy asked, "May I pray with you?"

I thought, *What's a prayer going to do? Why not? It can't hurt anything.* "Yes," I said. So we got into my

Toyota FJ Cruiser, black with a white top, and there, parked out front of Garrison's restaurant, Amy prayed.

TWO

THE POWER OF PRAYER

"Submit yourselves, then, to God.
Resist the devil, and he will flee from you."
— James 4:7

As Amy began to pray with me while we sat in my car, I was in a low place emotionally. I desired to get rid of all of my past, all the confusion, the brokenness, and the emptiness. What started as sweet generic prayer shifted to a kind of prayer I'd never experienced.

Amy asked, "Do you mind if I take authority over the enemy that has taken over you?"

Having no clue what Amy was referring to, I agreed.

Prayer started coming out of Amy as if she were a commander in chief. I realized quickly I had a warrior next to me beginning to battle the gates of hell for my soul. I surrendered completely.

"Romans 10 says, 'For if you confess with your mouth that Jesus is Lord and believe in your heart that God raised him from the dead, you will be saved. For one believes with the heart and so is justified, and one confesses with the mouth and so is saved.' Repeat these words with me."

That day in my car, I spoke these words, "Jesus, You are my Lord and Savior. I believe You died on the cross to save me from my sins, rose again on the third day, and now are seated at the right hand of God the Father, in heaven."

We were at war for my soul. She forbid the enemy of my soul to manifest inappropriately and commanded the enemy to politely leave me. As the prayer shifted into high gear, I sensed masses—alive, gross, and stubborn—separate personalities of the enemy, spirits of evil, shifting within me, not wanting to release their hold on me as she commanded them to do. I shifted too. Everything that I had done, through the life I had experienced since my conception, was all coming to the front of my consciousness. A desire welled up within me; I wanted full release. I wanted these feelings, these spirits, to be gone!

One by one, Amy called out the very struggles I had been living through.

"Addictions, we see you. You must come out ...."

THREE

THE SEDUCTION OF ADDICTIONS

"For though we live in the world, we do not wage war as the world does. The weapons we fight with are not weapons of the world. On the contrary, they have divine power to demolish strongholds."
— 2 Corinthians 10:3, 4

With addictions, you don't set out to say, "Today I'm going to become a smoker, an alcoholic, a drug addict," or whatever it is you are struggling with. I had opened the door and allowed the strongholds of addictive drugs to come in. Seductions slowly take over. I remember saying, "One won't hurt me," and then one turned into two, and two turned into three, and so on. They enter slowly and soon take over.

I always believed I was in control. At different times, the addictions seemed stronger than others. It seemed they were knocking at my door daily; and, if I ran from them, they eventually found me again. I tried over and over again to quit, but I wasn't ready to let them go. When their control was most intense, I justified my behavior and continued to tell myself I didn't have a problem.

I wasn't brought up with alcohol or cigarettes in my home. I experienced them outside my home. I remember being curious, and I smoked my first cigarette down the street from my house in fifth grade. Soon a friend and I snuck cigarettes from her mother and went out to the woods to smoke. I thought it was disgusting, but at the same time we thought we were cool. I can even remember the commercials and how they imprinted on my thoughts that I'd be cool if I smoked. I didn't want anyone to know. I was torn, knowing I was not to be doing what I was doing yet feeling like a rebel and doing it anyway.

On a hot summer day after eighth grade, I was introduced to my first drink, Jack and Coke. Driving down a winding road in a gray Mustang with the windows down, singing loudly, "I Love Rock and Roll," I was with people several years older than I was who accepted me. Although this drink was a little much for me, I swallowed it. While I often did not feel accepted by my peers, these people made me feel like one of them.

Thinking about this now, what was an eighth grader doing drinking hard alcohol mixed with Coke? I know some start early, sneaking into their parents' liquor cabinet because they are curious, but what about those who provide substances to those under age? Do they have any idea they are contributing to forming these addictions? For many of us, these habits become huge issues.

That day we went to a friend's house, continued drinking, and that evening drove to a large parking lot. I remember getting out of the car, lying on the ground, looking straight up, and talking to the stars, realizing something wasn't quite right. I felt as if there was nothing I could do; I was paralyzed. The people I was with laughed, thinking it was funny, not realizing the path of destruction that had now begun. This was the first time I was drunk and was the beginning of what was to come.

I entered high school that fall, and I was faced with so much I wasn't prepared for: guys, flirting, parties, relationships, and sex, including alcohol, cigarettes, drugs, and all that came with that. The desire to fit in seemed foremost; and, although I was running varsity cross country, that didn't take away the desire to go to parties. As I socialized, I felt peer pressure to drink, which led to guys, and on from there. From the first time I tasted beer, I couldn't stand the smell. The more parties I attended, though, the more I learned to drink beer or whatever someone was offering. I learned quickly to smoke a cigarette; smoking helped take away the taste of the beer. I knew the choices I was making were not how I was raised. I remember feeling guilt and shame while doing them and realizing I was hiding so much from my mother, my friends, the guy I was dating at the time, my peers, my coaches and teachers, and my church family.

I remember feeling insecure from a young age. I lived in a single-parent home and my mom did the best she could, but at times we didn't have electricity, running water, a telephone, and other basic necessities. Occasionally, the church brought us food. I know now it was a gift from God, but at the time I didn't see it that way. I was embarrassed. I used my social life and alcohol to hide from the reality of what was going on at home. I wanted money, nice clothes, and nice shoes. I wanted to be perceived as someone different than I was. I had always been energetic, had always had a positive outlook despite my inner torment, and had always been good at most things that I tried, but that's not how I viewed myself. Often I compared myself to whoever was around me, always feeling inferior because I didn't have what everyone else had.

I remember being embarrassed while smoking around people who were not smoking. I was ashamed of what I was doing, not only because I was taught it was wrong but also because of this stigma of what others thought of people who smoke. The label seemed to be, "If you were smoking around other smokers, you were cool; if you were smoking around non-smokers, you were looked down upon."

Whether it was smoking pot before school or skipping school for an hour during the day to get high and come back, I used drugs more in my sophomore year. A close friend I had been dating announced he was leaving to go back to prep school in another state. My mom lost her job. My family lost the house I had been living in since second grade, and we moved into a house where I didn't feel safe, didn't want to sleep, and didn't want to live. These things happened, and I had no control over the decisions being made. I was furious and angry at the world and everything and everyone I came into contact with. If you crossed me, watch out. I was escaping by going to that place of getting drunk and/or high.

That same year I skipped school during fifth hour one day and took shots of peach schnapps over by a golf course. I came back to school so drunk I fell in the hallway after asking my math teacher if I could use the bathroom. That same day I had track practice. Instead of going around a fence, I crawled under it to save some time and tore a huge gash in my leg. I had no idea until someone told me I was bleeding because I couldn't feel it. I was struggling in the midst of a drunken fog and trying to stay above water. I was hiding at every turn while continuing to starve for a love I searched for but couldn't find.

Although I was friends with many people, I felt as if I never fit in anywhere. Many would be shocked to hear me say that. I enjoyed not being within one particular group because I wasn't attached. I didn't get too close to anyone, so no one really knew me and knew all that I was doing.

During that same year, I had a hard time running because of the smoking. On our way to the sectional track meet, I coughed up phlegm in chunks. During my race—the 2-mile run—I couldn't breathe, got sick, and had to drop out. I had just run the 5K in the state cross country meet the previous fall and should have made it to the state track meet in the 2-mile run. I didn't due to partying too much the weekend before the race.

This race was the end of my running career in high school. I went on to the next thing, being a pom-pom with the band. This brought many fun opportunities such as dancing during assemblies, being on the sidelines of football games, marching in band competitions (which I had been involved with since my freshman year), and marching in the 1988 Rose Bowl Parade. I was also now dating someone who was in college, who was five years older than me, and who played a fatherly role in my life. I felt more accepted because I was in front of the school and dating him. I was being steered away from the social groups that I had been hanging around, and I was now back in church. I was feeling better about myself, but my reality was that I was getting ready to learn how to live between two worlds: I learned how to live with one foot in the church and one foot out of the church.

Although I didn't have any trouble finding alcohol at this time in my life, knowing him opened up more doors to being served alcohol since he was 21. Along with this relationship came a new social group, his college-age friends. Several of them were doing drugs. Several times I was provided with pills, pot, shrooms, and things I didn't even know what they were.

What I remember is that I hid my smoking from him, yet there were times in our dating when he let me smoke due to the social circumstances. I was 15, 16, 17 years old hanging around 21-, 22-, and 23-year-olds, some of whom dealt drugs. I pretended it was OK because I was with my boyfriend and because I was with older guys. I was blind to the influence these people were having on me.

I remember I was invited to one of their houses and my boyfriend would be over after he got out of class. I was given pills of some sort. I acted like it was no big deal because I wanted them to accept me and think I was cool. I took those pills, smoked pot, and drank. By the time they asked if I wanted a shot of tequila, I took the shot and started hyperventilating. I couldn't breathe, and they laughed. When the guy I was dating showed up, I was trashed and he was very upset with me.

Bottom line: it happens slowly, and then you find yourself amongst company who are not trying to help you but who are influencing to ruin you. Just because they say they are your friends doesn't mean they are. I struggled for some time with how I presented myself, hiding what I was doing, pretending what I was doing wasn't being seen, and trying to be careful about who knew what.

After that guy and I broke up during my senior year, I turned back to church and God, wanting to live a life of innocence and purity. I was in a work study program for a prestigious organization, on the honor roll, hadn't skipped a day of school that year, and was trying to pull my life together. I stopped drinking for a time and spoke in front of my church youth group about the struggles I faced with the alcohol, drugs, relationships, and cigarettes. I was searching for more.

Within weeks I was back with a group of high-school girls, going to bars, and buying beer at a pizza establishment. The enticement and lure were strong. The thrill of being able to buy beer, get into the bars, and hang out with the older crowd was exciting. I was only 17.

In college, parties and alcohol were socially acceptable. Attending an all-women's school near a prominent, formerly all-men's school, I was on another playing field. Judgment was heavy. I learned to put on an even bigger front. I presented myself as having it together. I worked on campus and gave tours, was freshman class president, and joined a sorority.

I had gone to college to make a fresh start, but I found alcohol, drugs, guys, and cigarettes. I struggled with finances, insecurities, and guilt from returning to the things I was trying to stay away from. Drinking became my escape along with occasionally smoking pot. I would sometimes be completely out of control. I enjoyed letting loose; but, at the same time, I did not like the feeling of being out of control. My decision-making process changed and became irrational at times. I often drove to parties by myself. When I was ready to go, I would slip out, at times never telling anyone I was leaving. I liked being free to come and go, not being attached to one particular group. When I did, people would judge me.

Many times I was drunk at a party and decided to leave on a whim—whether to go to multiple parties in the same night or to drive five hours to see a boyfriend unannounced and then drive back. I would go over the details of the previous night, beating myself up for leaving my friends, driving drunk, and being intimate with whomever I was with at the time. I continued to make poor choices when I knew what I was doing was wrong.

The very things I was doing were molding the person I was going to be for the rest of my life. Someone might say, "What's the big deal if you're not hurting someone else?" The problem is the decisions I made affected those around me. I hurt a lot of people, and I remain thankful I never crossed anyone's path while I was driving drunk.

During my sophomore year in college, I entered AA. I remember going 19 days without a drink. After 19 days, I looked around the room. I didn't see anyone who looked like me and convinced myself I was fine. So after 19 days I stopped going to AA. I told myself, *I am in college, having a good time, and everyone is doing it.*

I graduated from college. I believed the social life was the life to have—going to pre-parties, to parties, then to after-parties. I always had a drink in my hand. It became liquid courage for me. I could be friendly to

anyone; I was more outgoing with it. This is who I had
become.

At times I said, "No." I tried to do the right thing.
Unfortunately, depending upon whom I was with or
who came across my path, I sometimes still ended up
in a place to do pills, pot, cocaine, or other drugs. Even
though I said no, just by someone asking me again or
even being in the place where drugs were present, I
would eventually give in.

I went out with a girlfriend in New York, drinking
after smoking pot. Between bars in her car in a parking
lot, she asked me if I wanted to do a line of cocaine. I
ended up doing two lines of cocaine. Later I tried to go
to sleep but couldn't. I heard the song, "In a New York
Minute," playing on the radio. Drunk and high, I cried
out to God, "If You let me wake up, I will never do this
again," begging Him to take me out of this place. I was
afraid I wouldn't be able to come out in time. As I
listened to that song, so many thoughts ran through
my head—disappointment in myself, wondering how
I got to this place. I finally fell asleep. That next day,
although hung over, I was not in the same state of
mind I had been in the night before. I was relieved. At
the same time, I was angry at myself. I wanted to quit
doing these things, but I didn't know how... and I
wasn't ready to give them up.

I continued to be "social," as I called it. Relationships were difficult and often came down to the issue of trust. I married and soon realized both of us had alcohol issues. I recall one reason I was with him was because he did not hold me accountable. I could act how I wanted and say what I wanted. My mouth was not fit for silver and china.

My dream was to marry in a church with my family and friends beside me and be in love with someone who would think I was the greatest thing since sliced bread. I wanted to be pursued and be surprised when I was proposed to. Reality was there was so much anxiety because our relationship had been hidden from all but a few close friends. Shortly after moving in with him, I found out I was pregnant. We chose to keep the child and get married.

I made sure everyone saw my ring and heard of our wedding in Jamaica and our trip to Utah to honeymoon by snow skiing with his friends. But I wasn't proposed to; I didn't plan my wedding with my mom, picking out fabric and napkins for my wedding; my mom didn't make my dress or bridesmaids' dresses; I didn't have a church wedding; and no one but the minister, my husband, and the resort-supplied witnesses saw us get married.

This marriage was tough from the get-go. I continued to feel guilt and shame for my choices. Early in our marriage it was evident that being married wasn't the number one priority. Our marriage was based on lies, alcohol, and not knowing each other.

I made the best decisions I could make at the time, but the decisions I had made earlier had shaped the person I had become. I felt stuck; I didn't know what to do but try to do the right thing for my baby.

We kept up the illusion we were happy, each with successful careers. We had a nice home, new cars, and finances in reserve. We had another baby, a girl. The house was spotless; the laundry was done. I got the kids ready for daycare, dropped them off, worked and traveled, fixed dinner, bathed the kids, put them to bed, and then stayed up until midnight or later trying to do all I needed to get done. We were in church every Sunday. When I traveled for my career, I made sure I did not compromise my marriage and family.

People didn't see the arguments and struggles with alcohol, the hate and anger, the disappointments, and the lack of friendship, feeling at times like we were roommates passing each other as we traveled for our careers. Heartache was apparent. Our relationship was filled with broken trust, a lack of faith, and a lack of love, and did not center on God. While we went to several counselors for a couple years and tried to resolve these issues, our struggles with alcohol had devoured our marriage. We divorced.

Through my divorce and for several years afterward, I continued to struggle with alcohol. I went out on weekends as if I had been set free—going to concerts, to bars, to the lake during my time off from the kids. My comfort was being alone next to my fireplace with a pack of cigarettes and a beer, a glass of wine, or a mixed drink. I felt safe there. I would awake at two or three in the morning, realizing I had passed out from too much to drink. I would set my alarm to get the kids up for school and get ready for work and put on my mask for the day. I focused on my career and became involved in the community and my church, pouring and extending my energy outward so I could avoid looking at myself.

I continued seeing our counselor after our divorce and eventually started seeing a psychologist. I wanted confirmation I wasn't crazy. Due to anxiety and anger, I found myself on 250 mg of Wellbutrin and Zoloft, both antidepressants. I continued to drink. I was hurt from my divorce.

In 2006, I stopped the anti-depressants cold turkey. I tried unsuccessfully to quit smoking and drinking to train for a half-marathon that August in Virginia Beach. I thought this would be exciting; my running was something I lost once I married and had children. While running this half-marathon, I thought it would be funny to prove that I could drink and run at the same time. I did. As my friends and I completed this race, talks were we were going to do a full marathon that next year. How was I ever going to run 26.2 miles while smoking, drinking, and not training properly?

I was tired of living a lie, putting on a front, and not being honest with myself or anyone. I didn't know what love was, and I didn't believe I'd ever receive love. I just wanted to get out of the hell I had been living in.

FOUR

THE POWER OF PRAYER – SPIRIT OF ADDICTIONS BROKEN

"Therefore I tell you, whatever you ask for in prayer, believe that you have received it, and it will be yours."
— Mark 11:24

"Addictions, you are not welcome here any longer, and you must go in the name of Jesus," Amy said. When she spoke, I was instantly in tune with her, on board, in sync, and obedient to follow her direction. Still sitting in my car, I was listening, waiting, not knowing what was about to happen. I was in tune with my body and this scurrying of these masses, not knowing how many were present but wanting them all out of me. Immediately, I could feel a mass in my forearm. I grabbed her right hand and placed it on my right forearm where I could feel this mass, and said, "It's right here."

She continued renouncing this spirit, warring in prayer, speaking to it directly multiple times, for it to come out of me. I could feel this thing starting to be drawn out from the core of my body. As I exhaled, this mass began to come out. It did not want to release itself. Even though I had just eaten lunch, I was not throwing up food; I was purging the very enemy that had control over my soul. As I continued to exhale, over and over, I gasped for air, unable to breathe, feeling as if my airways were blocked by this mass that Amy was drawing forth with the help of the Holy Spirit. Finally, the spirit of addiction was completely out of me. Without her telling me, I knew it was gone.

From this point on, I was fully aware there were still more spirits inside of me and they were hiding to not be caught. They had been found out, yet they didn't want to leave. I looked at Amy with a trust I have never had before with someone. I submitted to what was next. I took a breath and said, "Let's keep going."

I felt movement in my stomach. When I told her, she asked if she could lay hands on my stomach. She then called forth the spirit of abortion. I thought, *How did she know?* I had aborted three babies.

FIVE

THE LIES OF ABORTION

*"A voice is heard in Ramah, mourning and great
weeping, Rachel weeping for her children and refusing
to be comforted, because they are no more."*
— *Jeremiah 31:15*

I don't believe anyone sets out to become pregnant to
have an abortion. Through decisions and
circumstances, women find themselves pregnant and
ask, "What do I do now?" I was in this place multiple
times. I never imagined sharing this area of my life
with anyone privately, let alone publicly.

From an early age I yearned for a male's attention.
Although I was raised in a Christian home, learning
biblical principles, including waiting until marriage to
give myself to someone, I was in sexual relationships
as early as my freshman year in high school. In my
junior year, I thought I was pregnant. The guy made it

very clear what we would do: "For us to make sure you're not pregnant, go to the doctor to have a pregnancy test. If you are pregnant, you will have an abortion." We were both concerned about our reputations. I knew nothing about having an abortion. I had no money and no insurance, and I remember thinking, *What will I do if I am pregnant? Will I have to drop out of school, and then what will I do?*

I made an appointment, he gave me money for the doctor's visit, and he dropped me off. I sat in the doctor's office by myself, waiting for the news. The doctor entered the room and told me I was not pregnant. I felt complete relief come over me. My selfish desires took over, and all I could think about was that the fun was not going to stop and I could go back to what I had been doing.

When the guy picked me up, the anticipation of whether I was pregnant or not was on the tip of his tongue. When I told him I wasn't pregnant, I could see the relief on his face. His only response was, "We need to be careful."   I didn't hear, "I love you," or, "Are you OK?"   The love I thought he had for me seemed to disappear that day.

Trust was a huge barrier in our relationship. I realized there were more things about him I didn't know, and there were things about me he didn't know. He wasn't aware of the issues that I faced economically at home. I remember always feeling embarrassed. My insecurities would come to the forefront, and I wasn't honest with how I was living my life. When I wasn't with him, trying to be the girlfriend I thought he wanted me to be, sometimes I was doing things he wouldn't approve of. Still, I always wanted to feel like he was taking care of me. I often placed him in a fatherly role because of his age and his portrayal of always having it together. I hadn't had a relationship like that before. Thinking I was pregnant and then finding out I wasn't brought hurt and hesitation into our relationship. I was scared I wasn't good enough.

As a junior in college, I met a guy at the Lake of the Ozarks while out with my friends one hot summer night. He was a pilot and had just graduated from college. We started dating, and I was in a sexual relationship with him. Within several months, issues with trust, distance, and drinking developed. That next spring, after dating long distance, I knew something wasn't right. Immediately, I called my girlfriend 30 miles away with the concern I might be pregnant. Knowing what she had told me about pregnancy, I felt many of the same symptoms. I asked her to bring me a pregnancy test to where I was in college. I lived in a sorority house, and I didn't want any of them to know. As we sat outside my sorority house, smoking cigarettes and laughing, I was scared of what I was going to do if that test came back positive. After my friend left, I took the test. The lines showed up really fast. I was pregnant. Trying to remain calm, I called my friend and said, "You're not going to believe this. I'm pregnant. What am I going to do? Maybe you should bring me another pregnancy test."

She said, "Just calm down, and let's think this through."

"What am I going to do? I can't quit school. My mom will kill me."

"Susan, everything is going to be OK. No one needs to know, and you can go have an abortion. It's not that big of a deal."

"Where do I call? Who do I talk to? What is my boyfriend going to say, and how am I going to tell him?"

How *was* I going to tell my boyfriend? I wondered if he would break up with me after finding out. He lived in a different state. Was I going to live with him? I didn't want to quit school. How would I pay for an abortion? How would I pay for a baby?

I called an abortion clinic. I was asked basic information: name, address, and the date of my last menstrual cycle so they could determine how far along I was and how much it was going to cost. I was told, "Bring someone to drive you home. The procedure won't take long. It may be a total of 10 minutes. You will be groggy and tired afterward, but within a few days you will feel normal again. The surgical procedure is safe, and people have it all the time. Bring $350."

I asked, "No one will ever know?"

She assured me, "No one will ever know."

As I got off the phone with the clinic, I called my boyfriend. I told him I was pregnant and had called an abortion clinic to get options. We quickly decided I would have an abortion. I scheduled the appointment. I would drive to Tulsa in a few weeks, meet him, and then leave Saturday morning to drive to the abortion clinic near Norman, Oklahoma.

During the five-hour drive by myself from mid-Missouri to Tulsa, I had time to think. I felt awful, and I knew the life inside me was real. I was scared and felt alone, never discussing many details with my boyfriend. I put on a tough act. That defense mechanism protected me many times up to this point. I was in control, I made myself believe, and I wanted everyone else to believe it too. What could hurt me worse than I had already been hurt? No way was I going to have a baby. I was going to be successful at my career, and a baby would get in the way. Only with my best friend, whom I told everything to, did I discuss that I was pregnant. Although cigarettes tasted gross,

I smoked to take the edge off and hide the reality of what was going on inside my body.

I recalled stories of my girlfriend's sister being a pro-lifer in Steubenville, Ohio, where she went to college. She would get arrested for chaining herself to the doors of abortion clinics so people could not get in. We laughed at her and thought she was crazy, so the pre-warnings I received from the clinic and the ideas I had of what to expect circled in my head. I arrived late that night. My boyfriend and I got up early the next morning and drove to the clinic. I wasn't mentally and emotionally prepared for the experience.

I felt ashamed as I walked up to the clinic door. Protestors were outside. I was told to put my head down and keep walking. How could they understand?

I filled out paperwork. I was taken back for counsel. I was asked questions to confirm how far along I was. While I was literally shaking, she convinced me I was making the right choice. Not once was I counseled that this tissue was a baby, alive and living, with a beating heart. She told me my problem would be taken care of that day and sent me back to the waiting room. Time seemed to stand still.

A nurse led me to the surgical room. She reviewed the procedures. She was not using words such as *abortion* or saying, "You are killing your baby." She spoke to me in terms of terminating a pregnancy and removing tissue.

I undressed and put on a robe. The doctor explained to me what was going to happen in this procedure. I would be given medicine. I wouldn't feel much of anything, except for a pinching sensation in my abdomen. The procedure would only take 5 to 10 minutes. I was told I would have some cramping, bleeding like a menstrual cycle, but that within a few days I would be back to normal. I was advised I should have a follow-up visit. I thought, *I'll be just fine.* I was afraid they would not let me have the abortion if I told them I couldn't make it back for a follow-up appointment because I lived out of state.

This wasn't what I was taught to do. I knew I was taking a life that God had placed on this earth. This seemed to be the only rational decision if I wanted to amount to anything. I went to an all-women's college where status and money were everything. How would I ever achieve any of that if I were barefoot and pregnant?

They asked, "Do you have any further questions before we proceed?"

I answered, "No." I just wanted to get it over with. As tears ran down my face, the woman next to me held my hand as they proceeded to prepare my body and use the surgical tools and suck the life out of the inside of me. I never felt so in control, yet so out of control. I thought, *What am I doing, how did I get to this place, and how can God ever forgive me?* Immediately condemnation covered me, and guilt and shame clothed me. I felt sadness and grief.

I was tired, drugged up, sore, and exhausted mentally and emotionally. I slept the entire way back to Tulsa. When we arrived back at his parents' house where we were staying, I remember him getting upset because I didn't want to wake up. Finally I walked into the house, went into the room where I was staying, and all I could do was sleep. The life had been taken out of me. I had no energy. I felt empty. He was so irritated with me, which in turn made me feel sad, angry, and alone even though he was right next to me. What was happening to our relationship? I felt this separation from the person I was relying on. I felt this intense void inside me. I wondered, *Who can I really trust, and who really loves me?* Depression hit me. I woke up several hours later, trying to act as if everything was normal.

I left that next day to drive to school, trying to act as if nothing had ever happened. I was going to be just fine. Back at school I went back to my habits, feeling relieved but rejected and unloved. Over several weeks, my already insecure self became even more insecure with feelings of doubt and a lack of love, especially toward the relationship I was in. I continued trying to fill that void of love by partying, drinking, and socializing, but internally I withdrew emotionally. Did anyone know what I had done?

I made a pact with myself to continue following what I had learned since birth: If you don't talk about it, it doesn't exist.

I remained in that relationship. It hit many rocky roads of strife, mistrust, anxiety, lack of feeling love, giving love and receiving love, lack of companionship, insecurities, and questioning motives, with stress and drama. We couldn't get on the same page. I graduated from college later that year and accepted a job in Tulsa. I began my career and moved to where I had no family, yet to be where my boyfriend was. As months passed, our insecurities and issues took over and we broke up. I was devastated. I was obsessed and didn't know what I would do without him. I had become dependent on a false sense of security. He immediately started dating. I could not understand, after all we had been through, how he could just leave me. Months passed and then we got back together. I wasn't sure if it was because I begged or cried, or because of manipulation, or both. I hoped things would be different, but they weren't. Within months, I was pregnant for a second time.

The immediate decision was I would get another abortion. I would need to take off work, so I scheduled the appointment at a clinic in Tulsa. I told myself, *You'll be fine. You've been through this before, and it's going to be OK.*

He was not able to go with me this time, which meant he would not drive me home. The surgical abortion procedure required someone be with me to drive me home. I didn't know what I was going to do. I was tempted to tell a friend and ask if she would be willing to drive me home. I chose not to tell her; I did not want to expose myself.

When I arrived at the clinic that day, no people were standing outside on the sidewalk yelling. This building was unmarked, square, four-stories high, with tinted windows, dark, and with no sign to indicate it had an abortion clinic inside. Security was high, with several different checkpoints to get in. I was nervous about the doctor and these people, wondering what I had gotten myself into and why this place was so hidden.

As I entered multiple sets of security doors, I came into the office and was asked to fill out the standard paperwork. The attendant asked me if this was what I wanted. This time, speaking softly, I said, "Yes, this is the decision I've made." She then asked me if I had someone with me or if someone was picking me up. When I said no, she hesitated and said I would need to reschedule my appointment. With much convincing, I assured her over and over again that I would be just fine if I could just lay there for a while so I could sleep off the drugs when the procedure was over. She left the room.

I felt betrayed and angry, having to convince the abortion clinic to let me have an abortion. I was alone. I thought, *Surely, if he loved me, he'd be here with me. What kind of boyfriend would make me do this, not just once but twice and now by myself? What kind of relationship am I in? He doesn't love me. How could he?* I asked these questions as my mind played with me. This time I wasn't feeling confident in my decision; feelings of abuse and sadness fell upon me. I was doing this for a second time while feeling the guilt and shame of having made another mistake. I convinced myself this was the best decision I could make. The attendant returned and told me they would allow me to have the procedure that day.

I was in a big room with dim lighting that seemed like a science lab, so sterile with flat metal tables, old, and not up-to-date. It was cold. I was thankful I had socks on. I felt hidden, as if my being there was a secret. I wondered if this business was operating legally.

The woman who counseled me and brought me into this room where the procedure would be done asked me to get onto the table. The doctor introduced himself, and immediately pulled me down and positioned me on the table, putting my feet into stirrups and strapping them down to ensure I didn't move. As I lay in this cold, gray room, the woman sitting next to me holding my hand, I looked at her for reassurance. With tears flowing down my face, I could see she was so sorry but there was nothing she could say or do for me but hold my hand. As the procedure began, I heard the sound of the machine that was going to suck the life out of me. I felt the ripping away from the walls of my abdomen that was taking place. The doctor said, "It's almost over. Everything went OK. You will be just fine."

The procedure was over. I slept for almost two hours. I recall feeling groggy and tired while trying to pull myself together enough to act as if I was fine. I continued trying to convince them that no side effects remained and I would be fine driving home by myself.

Was I feeling regrets? I felt scared, alone, abandoned, tired, and abused on so many levels. I walked back through the multiple security doors. I couldn't walk very well. Exhausted from the surgery and still groggy from the drugs, I did all I could to stay focused while driving the four miles home.

Relieved when I made it home, I crawled into my bed, exhausted from all I had endured that day, alone. I cried, feeling the guilt, shame, and lack of love. How could I be in this place again and with no one to take care of me? Was this what I deserved after all?

My life was based on hiding and keeping secrets. Anger dwelled in me. I had taken two lives. What was my life worth? Why did everything seem so hard? Thoughts of taking my life came several times, but I knew that was something I couldn't do. I was taught that nothing could be that bad to take one's life. It was one of the most selfish things you could do, leaving your family behind to deal with the grief. That was not an option.

Months later, that relationship ended. I was searching again. I got approval to transfer with my job to work on a newer segment of the company. I escaped from the two years that had brought much heartache. I was ready to move forward. I arrived at my new location within 30 minutes of my hometown and automatically reconnected with people I had lost touch with. Within weeks, I met someone on the construction site I was on. I was back to socializing as usual. I ended up inviting this guy over. He wasn't someone I saw myself with for the rest of my life, but he was someone to fill the gap. I had an itch to go to a larger city and didn't know how long I would be staying. As we hung out, it was automatic to be with him. Yearning once again for that touch and desire to be loved, I gave myself to him. I wasn't in love with him and went through the motions, almost as if I were dead. Within three months of my arrival, I received a call for a position in Dallas and I would be moving soon. I was pregnant.

There is no way I'm having this baby and staying here in this small town with this guy, I thought. Within a short time of finding out, I found an abortion clinic in Dallas. I scheduled my abortion for the week I would start my new job.

I made it clear to the guy I was seeing that I would be getting an abortion once arriving in Dallas. I had no feelings for him. My career was ahead of me, and I wanted nothing to get in my way. This was my breakthrough for all I had gone through. My mind was made up. I could tell he was sad and didn't know what to do. I told him, "It's no big deal. This is the best thing and will be better for us both. I'm moving." I could feel he wanted to hang on to me.

He came to Dallas that week and went with me to have my abortion. Several protesters were outside this clinic. He was like a dog with his head down. I was confident. I kept my eyes focused on the door to get into that building. This time was different than the previous two because I had a plan. I was in Dallas with life in front of me, and nothing was going to get in my way.

The waiting room was filled with women of several races and age groups. I stood confidently next to this guy who was having a hard time. I said, "It's fine. You can go back home, and things will be good." I was thinking, *After today, all memory and evidence of us ever being together will be over.*

I felt no regret at the time, except for wishing I had never met him. I had no emotional attachment to him, and my heart was hard. Nothing was going to hurt me this time.

We went back to the apartment a girlfriend and I shared. I was tired, hurt, and angry deep inside. As I lay resting that day, I felt so ashamed of the person I had become. Realizing that the guy I had given my virginity to and the guys I had had the three abortions with all shared the same first name, I decided that name was marked off the dating list.

The questions remained. Would I ever be able to have children again after aborting three of mine? Would God forgive me for all I had done? I was not in a place of forgiving myself. Would I ever feel loved by anyone? Would there be someone who would want to marry me? I didn't know what love looked like, and I didn't know what a healthy relationship looked like. I didn't love myself, and I didn't know how to give and receive love.

Within two years I was in another relationship and found myself pregnant again. We kept the baby and got married. Twenty-seven months later we had our second child. While our two beautiful, healthy children had been—and still are—a blessing, the struggles which existed in our relationship took over. A few years later we separated and then divorced. I had never revealed the abortions. I shoved my turmoil into the deepest, darkest place it would go to hide it so that no one would find out—not even the man I married.

SIX

THE POWER OF PRAYER – SPIRIT OF ABORTION BROKEN

"If we confess our sins, he is faithful and just and will forgive us our sins and purify us from all unrighteousness."
                                    — 1 John 1:9

When Amy spoke these words of knowledge as she continued to pray, I wondered how she knew I had had abortions. Something great was at work. As release occurred, it was powerful because this secret is the one I had shoved to the deepest darkest place. As the Holy Spirit revealed exact words and descriptions to her, the power of the Holy Spirit was revealed to me in a way I had never known before.

With the power of the Holy Spirit, Amy, battling the devil and the gates of hell, drew the spirit of abortion from my womb. It felt as if the lining of my womb, where this spirit was residing, holding on for its life, was being ripped out. As with the spirit of addictions, the spirit of abortion was being drawn up and out through my mouth. This battle seemed to be stronger than the previous one. I heard Amy speak with authority, "I forbid you to act up. You will not manifest. You will leave decently and in order. Release her, in the name of Jesus."

I threw up the very spirit that had overtaken me and the lies the devil had spoken into me through the years: that I was unworthy to be loved, that each of the babies I had aborted was just a blob of tissue, that abortion was no big deal and everything would be just fine, that I would be better off, and that abortion would resolve these problems.

As she expelled every lie that had been spoken with the decisions to abort all three of my babies, the entanglement was releasing. After much discipline and perseverance, the spirit was released in full. The victory came. My throat was sore, my insides ached, and I slumped over in the front seat of my car. Healing had occurred, and I knew it.

My mind and spirit asked God to forgive me as the evil one was being evicted. After the spirit of abortion was released, I knew I was released and forgiven. The rejection in my life, even as early as being in my mother's womb, was broken.

Before Amy continued praying, I caught my breath. Two spirits had been broken off, but I desired for them all to go. I had no idea how many were left. It was as if Amy had been mentoring me and praying with me for years. I remained open to all the Holy Spirit was doing. We fought these spirits from hell, and they were forced to leave. The release was so intense. Tears of joy, amazement, and freedom fell.

We continued battling. "There's one on my back," I said, pointing below my neck. She said, "Witchcraft, you've been found out, along with all that has come alongside you—Ouija boards and anything else you've used. You've got to come up and out."

How did she know I had tried Ouija boards?

SEVEN

WITCHCRAFT

*"The coming of the lawless one will be in accordance
with the work of Satan displayed in all kinds of
counterfeit miracles, signs and wonders...."*
— 2 Thessalonians 2:9

As a little girl, I would run down the steep wooden
stairs of our old house in the mornings, knowing the
paper had come. I would check my horoscope, looking
for a glimpse of what my day might hold. We did this
as a family. For years I looked and searched for
something that might give me some hope for that
day—reading fortune cookies and playing with a
Magic 8 Ball. Who was I? Who was my father? Why
was my life such a mystery?

I went to church and learned God's promises and
basic principles such as, "I'm a child of God, and I was
created in His image," but I never grasped these
concepts. I knew I was to follow the 10

Commandments. They seemed simple enough yet were so difficult because they covered so much ground. One commandment I heard over and over was, "Thou shalt have no other gods before me." I had no idea we had created a false god by looking for answers outside of the Bible.

I had been taught about heaven and hell. I had an idea of what evil was. A *Tom and Jerry* cartoon I watched as a child depicted a good angel on one shoulder and a little devil on the other. My mind told me, *It's OK for you to do this. No one will ever have to know,* and also hearing, *That's not what you should do. You were told not to do that.* I wanted to be good, but I didn't always make the best choices. I wanted to be friends with everyone and didn't want anyone to be mad at me. Sometimes, in anger, I said things I should not have said. As early as third grade, at the beginning of each school year, I would pray, "God, please give me a do-over. Give me a new start for this year, and let everyone forget what I did last year."

What seemed so harmless, reading horoscopes, then turned into some friends having a Ouija board when I was in high school. I recall one chilly fall night going to the old house on Ware Street. The air seemed to be still; it was dark, quiet, and the field around the house was grown up in places. My friends tried to talk me into going into this old abandoned house. Given the many scary movies I had watched, no way was I going into that house. We split up, because I couldn't bring myself to go inside that place. As my friends went in, I felt the presence of evil. As I stood by myself in this field, hearing their voices and footsteps, I felt this warm brush of wind come across my face. That was it. During what seemed like hours standing there waiting, I questioned what I was seeing and feeling. Was it real? I was curious about the spiritual world the Bible talks about.

Scary movies were a trigger point for me. They took me to a place of the unknown. When I was in grade school, my older sister took me to see the first *Halloween* movie, on Halloween. When we got home, I had to go trick-or-treating by myself. I took my dogs because I was scared to death. There was a huge field next to our house, and I remember wondering who was watching me and what was going to come out to get me. I knew scary movies were made up, full of gruesome details and often brutal killings, but they often included hate, anger, jealousy, and many evil and demonic things. As the music would draw me in to each scene, I would find myself at the edge of my seat chewing my fingernails and waiting for something else bad to happen. After watching these types of movies, I would have bad dreams, break out in a sweat, and wake up screaming. In my twenties I stopped watching them.

Music had a similar influence on me. I enjoyed upbeat music. I would become full of energy, never really paying attention to the words I was singing. Slow music would bring me to a screeching halt and often remind me of the sadness and brokenness in my life. I would feel lonely, and think about what I didn't have and who I wasn't. I remember crying for hours, listening to the same song over and over. I lived in this place throughout my life, unaware that what my eyes were seeing and my ears were hearing was penetrating my heart.

While friends and I experimented briefly with a Ouija board in high school out of curiosity, in college I sat with my sorority sisters and a few friends for longer periods of time. I remained curious. We started by asking questions everyone knew the answers to to test if it was real. For example, what color of shirt do I have on? Name someone here today. The correct answers would come. We laughed, but we were dealing with an unknown source. As we went on, we asked tougher questions: Who was my last boyfriend? Are we in college? Was there a fire on our campus? The answers came and verified the source knew the answers. As we lightly placed our fingers on this piece on the board, we made sure no one was pressing or moving this piece to guide the answers. We were dealing with something outside ourselves. The questions continued: Who was my first boyfriend? Only I would have known the answer. What was the name of someone hurt in the fire on campus? None of us would have known the answer. The answers kept coming. We were curious to tap into the unknown and another spiritual world.

Whether our experiments with the Ouija board opened the door or the door was already open, this spiritual world manifested in other ways in our sorority house. Many heard unexplainable noises, especially on the third-floor deck, such as the sound of a soda can being rolled around in the attic and doors slamming with no wind in sight; seeing pennies show up and scoot across the floor; and feeling someone or something brush up against them when they were the only ones in the room. These experiences opened my awareness that there was more out there and made me more curious about this other world that seemed to be unknown, or was it?

A close friend from high school started learning Zodiac signs. When I dated someone new, I found out when his birthday was, called her, and she explained the sign and supposedly who he was. She explained if he was going to be good for me and if our signs were compatible. Throughout college and after graduation, when I wasn't in a relationship, I called her when I met someone new. In addition to his birthday, she encouraged me to get the specific time he was born. She had multiple books she referenced. She made me aware of aspects of who he was, and I would either get excited or realize he was not going to work. I relied on her, these books, horoscopes, birthdays, etc., to give me the scoop so I could figure out who each one was and if he was the one for me. In time I thought of her as an expert. We'd laugh about it, and we began to share with others so they too would search. We wanted to know our destiny so badly that we relied on this information for truth. It didn't occur to me turn to the Word of God for answers.

Although witchcraft wasn't talked about in our church, I knew there were things I was to stay away from. My curiosity had gotten the best of me and soon became an open door for false beliefs and words to be spoken into my life.

After I married, the focus shifted away from seeking information about guys I was dating and shifted toward our careers, our family, and acquiring things. During this time, the Internet was increasing in popularity, and I set up my home page to include daily news, the weather, e-mail, and my daily horoscope, believing that a horoscope could reveal some truth I was missing.

After much deception, I divorced. I was seeking answers and wanted to know what my future held. Although I attended church every Sunday, I heard a friend of mine mention she had attended a psychic party with a tarot card reader. I was curious. Then another friend said she had gone to a tarot card reader. The one who attended the psychic party had a party and brought in a tarot card reader for entertainment. Although the original psychic could not come, she sent one of her friends to do the tarot card reading. My friend having the party was uneasy that night and did not want her cards read. The rest of us lined up. I remember asking, "What's the big deal? Just do it." She did. We hung out that night, socializing, which consisted of drinking and drinking and drinking, and of course, I couldn't have a drink without a cigarette.

Although this psychic didn't say a lot that night, she said enough for me to believe she knew something more that I didn't know. If there was a way she could predict my future, I wanted her to tell me what was ahead.

I wanted to go myself, so I searched online for a tarot card reader. I was then referred to the original psychic scheduled for my friend's party. Since my friend had seen her before, I asked her to go with me to this woman's office about an hour outside of

Atlanta. I was scared yet filled with anticipation of what might be spoken to me.

I decided to go first. As I walked into her office, I smelled incense and saw crystals, unicorns, books, rainbows, and spiritual images hanging on the walls. Though her office was small, it was overdone with paraphernalia. I moved things out of the way to pull out the chair in front of her desk so I could sit. I wondered, *If people frequent her office, why isn't it presented in more of a lovely manner?* This lady, whose hands were covered with rings, talked about spiritual things. Although she was friendly, immediately I was on guard and uneasy. Was that because I was afraid she could see right through me and see the very weaknesses I had? Was it because I could feel this demonic force lurking in this place? She assured me she would have information from a spiritual realm.

She said a prayer that didn't seem right and didn't feel right. She asked the stars and moon to align, and called out names of things and spirits I had never heard of. I wondered where this information was going to come from.

She started verifying information and finally got to the point that what she was saying had some truth. She mentioned I was seeing three different guys, which was true, and she named off the personalities each had. How did she know? She knew I was divorced and had been in a difficult relationship. While she only spent a few minutes with me, she said enough that I believed in what she was saying. If she wasn't real, how did she know these things?

I went to her multiple times, searching for more information, but wondering if she was really revealing anything to me. The craziness she knew about my life made it seem as if she were a fly on the wall watching me, but she wasn't giving me any big answers. I told a few people I had been seeing a psychic, and they couldn't believe it. When they asked me why, I said it was entertaining. Actually I hoped she could tell me my future and then I would know all that was ahead.

If she had the answers, why did I remain in a place of wanting the answers? Where was I headed? What was my life going to be like? I never received the answers I was searching for, and she couldn't tell me what I wanted to know. Money was spent to try to fill the broken and empty places. What I hoped was going to bring truth only brought more questions, uncertainty, and pain.

EIGHT

THE POWER OF PRAYER – DEMONIC STRONGHOLDS BROKEN

"Do not turn to mediums or necromancers;
do not seek them out, and so make yourselves unclean
*by them: I am the **Lord** your God."*
> — *Leviticus 19:31*

"You need to repent of all that you have ignorantly opened yourself up to on the enemy's turf," Amy said. "You need to repent of all witchcraft that you have been involved with."

So I said, "I repent and renounce all witchcraft, Ouija boards, tarot cards, tarot card readers, daily horoscopes, and anything else I have done pertaining to witchcraft."

I was not aware that the prayers the tarot card readers had prayed over me drew in demonic spirits. The things that were outside of God's will for me had come not only into my life but into my body. In searching for truth by exploring witchcraft, wanting to be whole and wanting the hurt to go away, I had invited evil spirits to dwell inside of me to take over my life. I had basically given myself to the devil.

As she prayed, I realized she was speaking in tongues, using a language I did not understand. With discernment and listening to the Holy Spirit, she said, "Spirit of witchcraft, you must go in the name of Jesus."

This spirit began coming out. I was holding on to Amy and the presence of the Holy Spirit as this slimy seducer was being drawn out. I was being untangled from the web I had allowed myself to be lured into. The spirit of witchcraft had a strong grip, internally, mentally, and emotionally. I had invited this demonic spirit into my life and it had found a dwelling deep inside of me. I knew I had to pray, listen, and be attentive to how the Holy Spirit was moving. It tugged, pulled, and held on with all its might as she told it to leave.

The ripping from inside of me was agonizing. This one was roaring like a lion as it came forth. I felt a powerful force thrusting up and out from the core of my body multiple times. The lying strength of this one was trying to make me believe that Jesus wasn't stronger than it was, and I had crossed a line and all the repenting I was doing wouldn't be enough. The enemy wanted me to think it had legal ground. Thank the Lord, Amy was listening to the Holy Spirit, understood that deception, knew what to do, and kept praying. We pressed into the Lord and prayed for the breaking of this spirit. I felt this huge release and took a deep breath. I was alive.

Looking back, the difference between the tarot card reader's source of information and Amy's is clear. With the tarot card reader, nothing was resolved. When we seek anything outside of God's will, the enemy will lie, steal, kill, and destroy. If he can get us off track from the plan and purpose God has for our lives, he has won. If he can keep us in despair and feeling sorry for ourselves, then we cannot move forward to all the blessings God has for us. We stay entrapped by evil vices that have taken over our lives. Once Amy began praying, the Holy Spirit took over, bundling up the hurt, pain, anger, resentment, uncertainties, insecurities, and falseness, and removing them. Lies and lures were being exposed by the truth.

As each spirit was removed, the heaviness and entrapment I had felt for so long was leaving. Although

I knew there were more because I could feel them, I began to feel lighter.

We took a breath, and I was able to get ready for the expelling of the next one. We were still sitting in my new car, in front of Garrison's, in the middle of the afternoon. Physically, I knew we were coming to the end; emotionally, I was exhausted. My speech was weak, and my throat was sore. I was sweating, coughing, and wiping my nose. My black outfit was coated with evidence. Every inch of me had evidence of freedom. A peace became stronger within me as we proceeded. I was crying from relief. I had such happiness along with a feeling of repentance and great regret in reflection that I had made such bad decisions. Yet as we incrementally proceeded, a greater excitement grew; I knew something big was occurring deep inside me. I knew I was in a place of trust, and I could not deny how powerful this experience was.

"How are you doing?" Amy asked.

"Let's keep going," I replied.

Amy called out the next spiritual force. I heard, "Deaf and dumb spirit, I command you to leave. You have to go in the name of Jesus."

NINE

DEAF AND DUMB SPIRIT

"The enemy pursues me, he crushes me to the ground;
he makes me dwell in the darkness like those long
dead. So my spirit grows faint within me; my heart
within me is dismayed...
For your name's sake, LORD, preserve my life;
in your righteousness, bring me out of trouble.
In your unfailing love, silence my enemies;
destroy all my foes, for I am your servant."
          — Psalm 143: 3, 4, 11, 12

I struggled academically, emotionally, and physically, not able to stay focused. I wondered if these struggles were things I brought on myself, the result of bad choices, insecurities, and listening to words telling me I was dumb. I heard Bible stories about Jesus casting out demons, but—up to this moment in the car—I could not fathom that demons would be cast out of me and might have had an impact on my ability to learn, read, and communicate. Is it possible Satan was trying to destroy every area of my life so I would not reach the calling God had for me?

Since kindergarten, I had a hard time in school and was made fun of. When I was five years old, I ran to my older sister at school for her protection from the kids making fun of me. She would set them straight. But why were they making fun of me? Was I different?

Acceptance always seemed to be an issue, especially at school. In second grade we moved from Columbia to Jefferson City, and I was put into a public school where I was placed into a special reading class. I never understood why. Was it because I read slower than most? Was it my fear of reading in front of others? Because I was placed in this group, I always felt inferior to the kids who could read and who did well in school. I thought I wasn't smart enough to be with the other kids. I remember participating in a spelling bee that year and being one of the best ones in my class. How is it I could spell, but I wasn't able to read?

By third grade my mom moved me into a private parochial school. The class size was smaller; and although it was a Lutheran school and I was raised Southern Baptist, I was comfortable in my surroundings. Within weeks I took a placement test, and again I was separated from the mainstream classroom and placed into a special reading class. I felt inferior, dumb, and judged.

We were also taken to a different area of the building. I thought, *What am I getting out of this*? We were taught at a slower pace, so I was bored and unable to focus. I wanted to be in a normal class. I don't recall my classmates in the normal class saying much when we would leave for the special reading class or when we would return, but I remember feeling as if I was not at the same level as those in the mainstream class. I wondered what they were being taught that I was missing. When it came to geography, math, and spelling, I did well. Outside of class, I enjoyed and excelled in sports and band. I had several friends and just wanted to be like everyone else.

During my sixth grade year at that school, one teacher tended to make very direct statements: "Susan, you're so stupid." He would say, "Do you have to be so stupid? Why can't you understand what I am saying?" I not only struggled with thinking that I was stupid because I was in a special reading class, but now I had a teacher telling me I was stupid.

I also felt this way at church and during Sunday school lessons. I often did not answer questions due to fear that I would not have the right answer and would be judged.

I did excel in religion class and memorization along with memorizing verses at Bible camp. I could memorize a page of the Lutheran catechism in less than 20 minutes on the way to school and also spelling words and get an A most of the time. I understood maps and calculated distances when I was reading and studying. At test time, however, I would forget key concepts and couldn't figure out how to apply what I had learned.

After the first semester of my seventh grade year, my mom transferred me back to public school. I was in the mainstream class for the first time, but I always had a hard time in English class. By the time eighth grade came, I was back in a special reading class. Again, I felt dumb.

My freshman year wasn't any better. I didn't get along well with my English teacher, and I was sent to the principal's office often. I respected those in the office, including the principal and the assistant principal. They seemed to understand my struggles, and I was honest with them. Every time I was sent to the principal's office, however, I missed key concepts I should have been learning in class.

Everything surrounding my life was difficult, and I was just weeks into my freshman year. My mom lost her job, finances at home were tough, I lost my virginity, I was judged and bullied at school, and I started drinking. I ran varsity cross country that fall and struggled with feeling like I was fitting in.

In spite of my struggles in and outside of class, my algebra teacher made all the difference in the world. I respected him, and he respected me. As my coach from seventh grade summer track, he taught me not to give up. I didn't want to disappoint him, nor did I want to disappoint myself. Although he was stern, I respected and even benefited from his authority. When I was being bullied in the cafeteria or by my locker, he was someone I could trust. He was a safe haven. He believed in me and gave me hope.

During my sophomore year in high school, I took biology. I had to be at band at 6:30 a.m. before school and run cross country until 5 p.m., often falling asleep on the couch at 7 p.m. At times I didn't get my homework done. At other times, my mom would try to help me with it. At exam time, I couldn't remember the information from class, the homework, and labs. I failed my first semester and dropped out of biology class.

I skipped school to the point I could have flunked out by the end of that year. I was torn by a close relationship that ended unexpectedly. I struggled with that loss and with a lack of trust for guys in general. I had a hard time focusing because we lost our house, and I was embarrassed by where we lived. I stopped wanting to go to school—partly from being bullied and partly from not doing well academically. Looking back,

I wondered if my learning difficulty was from not being able to pay attention in class, not comprehending what was being taught, or from complete exhaustion.

Toward the end of my sophomore year, I tried out for pom-pons, part of the marching band, and was voted to be on the squad. This gave me an identity with my peers, changed my outlook on life, and helped my motivation. I felt like I was given a second chance for my junior year, and I was trying to pull it together. My actions had begun to change overall because I was in the spotlight, and I was concerned about what everyone thought of me. I tried to make good decisions, but I wasn't consistent. Why couldn't I gain balance? Were the pressures around me too strong? I struggled in school, occasionally skipped symphonic band classes, and dropped out of Algebra II and French. Where was my happy medium? Even though I was a pom-pon, my insecurities were still present and I struggled with my identity. Who was I, and why did I have issues being consistent? It's not that I didn't want to be that better person; it just seemed easier at times to go with the crowd than to go with what I knew was right. I continued doing whatever I wanted to and often didn't worry about the consequences. As a result of my choices, I was not placed on the pom-pon squad for the next year.

I met with my school counselor. He guided me, directed me, and got me focused on life after high school. To graduate on time, I was given the opportunity to take a class before school in economics and to take a correspondence course through the University of Missouri—Columbia. I needed to do lessons and mail them. Though I had already taken algebra and geometry, I would be enrolled in a remedial math class to be able to have enough math credits to graduate. I would retake a semester of earth science to get my last science credit. I was now ready to face my senior year.

The summer before my senior year, I started a work study program with Economic Development, Administrative Services, for the State of Missouri, and loved it. I worked for one of the directors and his assistant. I dressed up daily, had responsibilities, and was finally in a place where I was respected for my talents and abilities. My focus changed. I was earning money and being responsible. During my senior year, I never skipped a day.

That fall, I had a decision to make: Would I go to college? My mom never told me, "Susan, you are going to college," but I knew that's what was expected. All of my family was college educated. With my past record in school, how would I get there? I struggled all through high school and wasn't supposed to graduate.

Would I be able to meet college admission requirements?

I got on the honor roll that year while getting on track to go to college. I knew I needed a small-school environment, and I wanted to go to an all-girls school because I thought they were more prestigious. I visited William Woods and knew immediately that was the place for me. It was small, quaint, and they did what it took to help me get in. I was accepted on academic probation, finished my senior year of high school, and graduated with a 1.89. Technically, a 2.0 is required to graduate from high school, but I was permitted to graduate because of the additional requirements I met.

I was excited to go to college, but continued struggling with paying attention, taking tests, and understanding material. Unlike most college campuses, we were not allowed to miss more than three classes per semester. I entered as an accounting major and struggled from the get-go, trying to absorb the required information in a short time. I struggled with self-esteem and felt dumb.

The summer between my freshman and sophomore years in college, I worked at Yellowstone National Park. I went from wearing Laura Ashley dresses to cut-offs, T-shirts, beads, and hiking boots. I found myself as my own best friend. I met a part of me that I had never met before. Returning to college, after tie-dying my sorority shirts over the summer, I had a hard time re-adjusting to college life at this all-girls school. My outlook on social status had changed. I lost the focus I had during my freshman year and began skipping classes. I almost failed out of college the first semester of my sophomore year. I started looking for a way out. A friend told me about her experiences as a nanny on the East Coast, so I called nanny agencies and was offered a position with the owners of a nanny agency in New York. I went to New York to try to pull myself back together.

No matter where I went, I dealt with who I was, what I wanted, and who I wanted to be. I ended up being there only four months. I lived in a large home on Long Island Sound, drove a Mercedes, and lived the life of the help, but I did not want to be treated like the help. I realized if I ever wanted anything in life, I would have to get an education. I enrolled back in school.

Had I gone right back to school from being a nanny in New York, I would have struggled, not having time to transition between the two. As it was, that summer I trained with a dear friend to ride our bikes in Ragbrai, a bike ride across Iowa. I got a job at my former church's daycare, and worked and rode that summer before returning to school. I reflected on the extremes I experienced the past year-and-a-half: the oneness with nature at Yellowstone and the materialistic world of Long Island Sound. I struggled to find common ground between both. For me to choose those destinations in the future, I needed to get in school, then work, and have the finances that would bring freedom to travel between these different worlds.

I returned to school that fall and switched my major from accounting to interior design. I was doing something I had never done, drafting, which seemed to come naturally. However, I struggled again in test taking and ended up taking several classes twice.

My goal my last semester was to have a job before I graduated. I persevered, calling every design firm in Tulsa. Six weeks before graduation I received confirmation that I had a job and would be moving to Tulsa. I had a job with a commercial design firm, but I still needed to graduate.

I needed certain grades to walk the stage. I met with my teachers, which I had been doing throughout that semester, to make sure I was on track to graduate. By the grace of God, I graduated. No more school.

That wasn't quite the case. Many think being in interior design is a joke, but this is serious stuff, especially when dealing with codes and specs, electrical and plumbing. To become licensed in interior design, I had to have two years practical experience to be able to take the National Council for Interior Design Qualification (NCIDQ) exam, a certification test almost like the CPA exam for accountants. After two years, I applied to take the exam. Then, I chose to take a class to prepare to take the exam.

Words spoken to me weeks before my graduation kept running through my head. One of my professors said, "Susan, you will not be able to pass this exam. It's too difficult. At the least, you will need another English class to be able to help you write the contract documents that are involved."

Graduating from a smaller program, I was intimidated by those who had graduated from interior architecture programs at major universities, knowing they had educational experience much more vast than mine.

I took the exam in Dallas. Within six months, I moved to Miami. I received the test results: I had passed two of the six sections. Although disappointed, I was excited that I had passed the building codes section, which meant I could be a licensed designer in the State of Florida. Over the next couple years and three states later, I took that exam four more times to pass the remaining sections. Through perseverance, I did it.

I thought, *I am an adult, still struggling through school and test taking. What is the problem?*

I had difficulty grasping general concepts. I had never read a whole book up to this point in my life. I read stories from my Bible since I was a little girl, but they did not make much sense to me. Was I dumb? Were all the things I had been told by my sixth grade teacher and again by my college professor true? Although educated, I felt uneducated compared to others with college degrees.

I learned to mask feeling dumb by portraying confidence, getting involved, dressing the role I was trying to fill, and building accomplishments— freshman class president and other leadership positions, sorority membership, college graduate, NCIDQ-certified interior designer, management positions, and titles behind my name. These things brought me worldly wealth and were signs of my success, but they did not fill the void I struggled with.

My lack of confidence in my ability to learn influenced not only my respect for myself but also my respect for those who taught me and those in authority. When teachers gave up on me, I was angry, disrespectful, and resentful. When teachers did care, I found it difficult to ask for help and often wanted to give up. Deep down inside there was always perseverance and hope. I wanted to be better and

different than I was. What kept holding me back? Was
a deaf and dumb spirit keeping me from God's purpose
and will for my life?

THE POWER OF PRAYER – DEAF AND DUMB SPIRIT BROKEN

*"The Spirit of the Sovereign LORD is on me,
because the LORD has anointed me to proclaim good
news to the poor. He has sent me to bind up the
brokenhearted, to proclaim freedom for the captives
and release from darkness for the prisoners, to
proclaim the year of the LORD's favor and the day of
vengeance of our God, to comfort all who mourn, and
provide for those who grieve in Zion—to bestow on
them a crown of beauty instead of ashes, the oil of
joy instead of mourning, and a garment of
praise instead of a spirit of despair. They will be called
oaks of righteousness, a planting of the LORD for the
display of his splendor."*

— Isaiah 61:1-3

When Amy called out the deaf and dumb spirit, it listened. Compared to the previous spirits, which put up quite a struggle, this one came out with more ease.

I was amazed at how much I had been struggling with, how much she was recognizing, and how much the Holy Spirit was showing her. Learning and reading had always been difficult for me. It was now evident that if the enemy could keep me focused on what I could not do, both using thoughts in my head and words spoken into my life to try to convince me I was not smart enough, then I would not accomplish the calling God had placed on my life.

As each one was released, I was aware of a void that remained where that spirit had resided inside of me. Some felt larger than others. The core of me was changing, not just spiritually but also physically. When this prayer began, my heart was like lava rock, hardened and full of holes, with jagged edges, set afire by anger, hatefulness, disappointment, and sadness for myself and others. My heart now felt like a soft mound of clay being reformed. I felt the release of pain and strife, and I realized that it wasn't over and I wanted *all* that He had for me. I remained submissive to Amy's direction and the Holy Spirit's leading.

Because this spirit came out more quickly than the others, we did not take a break after this one was released. Amy said, "I take authority over and I bind all soul ties that are not of God, and I command you to release her in the name of Jesus."

This was huge. Giving myself to guys while searching for love had become a way of life for me. I was tired of all the heartache and false pretenses. I was now ready to receive healing.

ELEVEN

SOUL TIES AND RELATIONSHIPS

"It is God's will that you should be sanctified:
that you should avoid sexual immorality;
that each of you should learn to control your own body
in a way that is holy and honorable,
not in passionate lust like the pagans, who do not know
God; and that in this matter no one should wrong his
brother or take advantage of him.
The Lord will punish men for all such sins,
as we have already told you and warned you.
For God did not call us to be impure, but to live a holy
life."
                                    — 1 Thessalonians 4:3-7

"You're adopted," my sister blurted out.

"No, I'm not!"

"Yes, you are!"

I remember running from the field at my grandma's house through the back door, passing through the utility room and kitchen, and into the dining room where I found my mom, jumped into her lap, and found much needed comfort. "What's the matter, Susie?"

"Weezie won't stop making fun of me, and she's telling me I'm adopted."

As I sat there and cried and cried, my mom hugged me tightly. Meanwhile, nothing was said to my sister, and no behavior was corrected with either of us. The truth remained a secret. I was four.

Throughout my life, I wanted to know who my father was. Why didn't I know anything about him? What was his name? His eye color? How tall was he? What did he do for a living? Who was this man I didn't know, and where was he? Did I know him? Did he live close? Did anyone know anything about him? Who was I, and where did I come from? I was never told anything about him nor was he ever discussed. This never made sense to me.

To fill the void of not having a father in my life, I was starving for attention at a young age. Since grade school, I chased boys and wanted a boyfriend. I had my first boyfriend in fourth grade. Ross, then it was Casey. I met them at church.

Within a few short years, I was in situations I should not have been in. As early as the eighth grade, I felt pressured to go farther physically than I wanted to go. The morals and values I was taught from a young age were tested. I was afraid a guy wouldn't like me if I said no; and when I did say no, he kept trying. I eventually started giving in, a little at a time. I didn't feel innocent anymore. I was now doing things I knew most other girls weren't doing. Shame and guilt followed me from those experiences. I was about to experience the ultimate place I knew I wasn't to go— giving myself to someone before marriage.

I was told I was mature for my age and had an old soul. I'm not sure if that was due to my hanging out with my sister's friends, who were all five years older than I was, or from going to a lot of activities with my mom and learning to communicate with adults. I wanted to be accepted by those older than I was, so I learned how to act so they didn't think I was a twerp.

During this time I was with high-school guys on band trips with my sister. I learned how to flirt. Guys flirted with me. Then these same guys gave that kind of friendly attention to other girls, and I didn't understand why. Often, my feelings were hurt.

Before I started high school, my grandfather died. He was the only male role model I had. I was Grandpa's girl; we shared a special bond. He nicknamed me "Monkey" because I liked to climb the sycamore tree outside their home. I climbed as high as I could until the top of the tree started swaying. Whether it was him tickling me, whiskering me on my face, or taking me for a ride on the lawn mower, I enjoyed spending time with him. After he passed away, I wished there had been more time with him.

Things changed quickly after his death. I went from being Grandpa's little girl to being a young lady making adult decisions in a matter of weeks. As I entered my freshman year in high school, I immediately felt pressure to fit in. There were so many guys to choose from. Running cross country and being in high-school marching band, I was constantly busy before and after school. I connected with a guy on my cross country team. I hung out a few times with him and his friends. Soon after school started, he took me home one Friday night after the high-school football game. We drove out in the country on a gravel road toward a friend of mine's home. He pulled over. One thing led to another, and I didn't say no. Before I realized what was really going on, it was too late.

In a split second it was over. I gave up the most sacred gift I had to give. I didn't really know this guy. I wasn't in love with him, and he wasn't in love with me. I knew I wasn't to be with someone like that until I married. I was disappointed in myself and so sad deep down inside for the decision I had just made, yet didn't feel like I had made it. I just did it. I had tears in my eyes, and it was obvious this meant nothing to him. No words were spoken. I felt taken advantage of. I felt nasty and ashamed. Why wasn't I guarding my heart?

By the time this was over, it was late. I didn't tell my mom where I was, and I didn't call because we didn't have a phone. By the time I got home around 11:30 p.m., she started yelling at me at my first step in the door, wanting to know where I had been. This was *not* a good combination. I had just slept with someone for the first time, was confused, alone, and had a million emotions running through my head, and now my mom was upset with me—for which I don't blame her a bit. My actions weren't respectful toward her. She thought I would be home soon after the football game, and I had never stayed out this late before. My actions were also not respectful toward me. I felt lost, disappointed in myself, and didn't know how to get back what I had given away—my virginity.

I didn't hear from him the rest of the weekend. When I went back to school that Monday, I felt as if I had this dark cloud over me and my insecurities went into overdrive. I felt like everyone was staring at me, and it seemed that everyone knew. Whether they knew or not, I felt this judgment all around me as if I had the scarlet letter *A* on me. Actually, it was more like an *X*, for X'd out and not a virgin anymore.

A few weeks later we went to homecoming together. This should have been a special time—my first homecoming, a freshman getting to go with an upperclassman, and dressing up. We didn't have anything to talk about, and it still felt like everyone was staring at me as if I had the plague. While I still saw him in cross country, we never dated after that night.

What should have been closure wasn't. Eventually, several people on my cross country team and a group of girls that were friends with him learned what had happened, and word spread. These girls did not like me. For the next several years, they made my life a living hell. When I say *hell*, I mean it. They ridiculed me—and my best friend when she was with me—at school, on weekends, and in any public setting. They got up on chairs in the middle of the cafeteria and screamed profanities at me. Their lockers were by mine. When I went to my locker, they screamed and yelled at me. One time when we drove my friend's mom's 280 ZX through the local hangout, McDonald's, they screamed and threw eggs at us.

I had no idea the decision I made to give myself to him would create a soul tie with him. I had given him a piece of my heart that would be tied with him and to him. Little did I know that my heart was now not whole, and this was the beginning of the scattering of the pieces of my heart.

My life had changed. I felt so ashamed I eventually stopped going to church. No longer a virgin, I wondered if it mattered if I decided to be with someone else. Because I was now marked, I wondered if good guys would even want to go out with me. I felt like an outcast, and really just wanted to fit in. I wanted to be loved. I started drinking and attending parties with people who were older than I was. I wanted to be a part of the social scene and be seen. The more I was involved and the more people would know me, the more I would be accepted, right?

I continued through my freshman year, partying, dating, and giving myself to a few other guys. The relationships didn't last. In algebra class, a friend said there was I guy she knew who liked me. Within a few months we became friends. Even though I was dating others, he obviously was interested in me. We became great friends and spent time together just hanging out, doing fun things. Sometimes we just sat and talked. I don't remember feeling pressure from him to be with him even though it was obvious he wanted to go out with me. I trusted him in a way I had never trusted anyone. I respected who he was, and I noticed he treated me differently. He always opened my car door and paid for everything. He dressed the way I liked. I met his family and looked up to them. They were respectable, classy people. I liked being with his family. Although I came from a different socioeconomic background, I felt at home—welcome, comfortable, accepted.

Several months passed. I felt so special, not used. He seemed to genuinely care about me and my feelings. I saw him standing on the track on several occasions with a huge smile on his face. He would watch me run. I wore a bright yellow T-shirt from church that had a huge smiley face on it that said, "Smile, Jesus loves you." That shirt tells of a time and place of such innocence, but my world was still shifting.

We often went to the track at the local university and hung out on the jump mat of the pole vault. We spent many evenings together—no pressure, just friends, until one day it clicked. He kissed me. My feelings changed in seconds. My eyes were opened, a friendship was built, and we had so much in common, especially music. We always listened to music and sang at the top of our lungs, laughing and smiling. Within weeks, summer came and we found ourselves alone, and I trusted him with my heart and was with him. With tears in my eyes and a love built over time, this seemed to be right and wasn't the way I had been treated in the past. There was a gentleness and a trust I held onto tightly.

I have no idea how we orchestrated all we did. I didn't have a phone at home, but I worked at Dunkin' Donuts. Somehow we arranged times for him to meet me at my house. When he would bring me home, he would sometimes ask why there weren't any lights on at our house, which gave me ample opportunity to say we didn't have electricity. Too embarrassed to tell him the truth, I would say my mom must be sleeping.

My fifteenth birthday came. He was so sweet, sending three dozen roses and six balloons to Dunkin Donuts where I was mopping floors and cleaning. I felt like Cinderella, and I never wanted that feeling to end. No one had ever treated me like this, and finally I had a boyfriend who knew how to treat me, so it seemed.

I really wanted to be myself in this relationship, but I continued to hide what was happening at home. It was near the end of June, and we were still without electricity. My sister had come home from college that summer, and we worked together much of the time at Dunkin' Donuts. During this time the water was shut off at home again because we owed $11. Although we had a well and were still able to have water, we did not have hot water for bathing and my mom did laundry by hand. My sister paid the water bill. I knew things were bad financially; I just didn't know how bad they were.

Within a few weeks, the guy I was dating took me to a party at Crown Center Farms, and Cool and the Gang was the band. Now this was in the '80s, so it was the coolest thing to go to this high-class party and be a part of this social crowd. As we walked around having fun, meeting several people and him knowing a few, I carried a fuzzy navel (that would be OJ and peach schnapps) and with it being an open bar, I drank and drank and drank. I grabbed the leg of one of the singers while he was on stage and wouldn't let go. I was drunk and out of control. After what had to have been at least 30 seconds, I suddenly realized what I was doing, knew I was not acting appropriately, became embarrassed, gathered myself together, and acted as if I hadn't done a thing. We continued socializing and then eventually left for home. As we drove the 40-minute drive back home, I puked out the car window.

The next day I remember feeling embarrassed and didn't actually know what had happened. Days went by, and I didn't hear from him. I was sad. I cried and cried for days, feeling like I had lost my best friend. Several weeks passed, and he finally contacted me to tell me he was leaving in a few weeks to go back to prep school along the East Coast. I was devastated. That evening was never discussed. I found myself in that place of feeling so alone and frustrated with myself for sharing so much and then ending up back in the same place. I trusted him with my heart and had spent so much time with him. How could it have just disappeared?

No one was communicating anything to me to help me understand what was going on. Shortly after he let me know he was leaving for prep school, we lost our house. It took me by surprise. How did I end up in the middle of this?

A few weeks before my sophomore year started, I began marching band and varsity cross country practice. Although the guy I had been seeing was now away at school, arrangements were made for me to stay with his family for a few days while Mom moved our things to a much smaller house. I felt desperate and was hoping he would reach out and be there for me. After Mom and I moved, which was close to the high school, I would walk over to the school at night to use the pay phone and use my sister's calling card to continue to reach out to him at school. Often I couldn't reach him. On the few occasions when I did, he had nothing to say. Why was I calling him? He had no interest in me, yet I couldn't let go. I did not understand how he could treat me so well for so long and then cut me off. I tried to remain focused in school, but I couldn't. I struggled with the music and hitting the marks on the field during marching band. I was getting yelled at all the time. My cross country running was good and I took second on our team at State, but it was suffering too. The pride I had in myself was fading along with my self-esteem. If only I had someone who believed in me.

That fall I wanted to escape. I had low self-esteem and had begun believing the lies I continued to hear at school. After the cross country and band season were over, I began skipping school, drinking and smoking more often, and doing drugs. I was gone from home most of the time, both at night and on weekends. I reached a point where I didn't care who I was hanging out with or what I was doing. I had no expectations of any of these guys at this time—a few of whom I gave myself to. I stopped going to church. This seemed to be one of the lowest times thus far in my life.

Since I was in grade school, I remember dreaming of becoming a pom-pon girl when I got to high school. Tryouts were at the end of my sophomore year. With the help of a friend, I tried out and made it. I truly believe this was the ticket that saved me from the bottomless pit I was falling into. I finally felt as if I was part of a group. I made some good friends. Other areas of my life started improving. I was selected for symphonic band, which was also an honor. On the home front we moved to a house where I felt a little more comfortable. Shortly after summer began, I began seeing a person who would play a fatherly role in my life.

I met him that spring, and he was five years older than I was. He was in college, and immediately I was attracted to him. He was handsome, appeared to have it all together, and had direction. He and a friend came to get me one evening. His parents were out of town, and they were having a barbecue. After drinking and hanging out for a while with his friends, the two of us were so attracted to each other that we took off on his motorcycle and drove out to the woods. We were both on a mission to be with each other. It's amazing what several beers will do to your thinking. I didn't know him, but giving myself to him and just being with him felt so natural. He knew who he was, he took charge, he was fun, and we were both adventurous. This whole experience was exciting.

Later that evening after everyone had left, the two of us were alone and the radio was playing. The song "Take My Breath Away" from the movie *Top Gun* began playing. I remember him saying that he had dedicated this song to me. No one had ever done anything like that for me. At the same time, as soon as that song came on, I was in complete shock and my eyes welled up with tears. As much as I wanted to be in the moment, all I could think about was the guy who gave me the roses and balloons when I turned 15. This song reminded me of a special moment we had had one night coming back from the lake.

My relationship with this college guy—as with most of the relationships I would be involved with from this point forward—would form completely backward: we would first be together sexually, then we would start hanging out, and then we would start dating and begin a relationship—not the way that I was taught in church: being courted, dating, getting married, and then being together sexually. There's something about getting to know someone in conversation and sharing life experiences together and just being friends. In this case, we didn't know much about one another and something significant seemed to be missing. Instead of feeling loved, I felt lonely and sad. I had just given a piece of my heart again.

After that night, I hoped the college guy would see me again. I didn't know how to define us. Due to me not having a phone, he was going to have to contact me. He did. He, his friend, and I spent that summer going to the lake, water skiing, hanging out, and partying together. Eventually we began dating. We ended up spending evenings together several times a week, hunting together, going to church on Sundays, and doing everything else in between. I fell in love with this guy and relied on him as I had never relied on anyone before. I had gone from high-school guys to being with someone older who seemed to have it all together.

Looking back, he played such a significant role in my life. I regained the importance of being in church and attending Sunday school while being surrounded by those of faith and who mentored me during this time. I understood the importance of presenting myself well in public. We would often go out to eat, and this is where I continued to learn proper etiquette, with him asking me what I would like and then him ordering for me, treating me like a lady. In the evenings, we would often study together, something I rarely did but which he encouraged. Eventually, he had me read Zig Ziglar's book, *See You at the Top*, which helped me believe I could do anything I set my mind to. On the flip side I found myself "in trouble" many times because of poor decisions that I would make, often due to consuming too much alcohol and getting out of control. Although I tried to hide these times of being out of control from him, believing he wouldn't like me if he knew the truth, I often seemed to get caught. While I wanted to be all that he wanted for me and wanted me to be, even appreciating the discipline at times, I found myself often rebelling at these things, missing my freedom. I had not had a male relate to me in a fatherly role as he did, and I didn't take to it well.

Because of the way our relationship began, trust always seemed to be an issue for us. Often, we would wonder what each other was doing when we weren't together. Our relationship started so spontaneously and fun. With my insecurities, I often wondered if he was having this fun with someone else or without me. He often asked me what I had been doing, which told me he had similar doubts. Halfway through my senior year, soon after Christmas, he broke up with me. I was devastated. That love I had had for him I had never experienced before. I felt lost, confused, and abandoned once again. My heart was shattered. Who would encourage me to stay on the straight and narrow path, caring so deeply about me, filling these roles that he had played so prominently in life?

During the next few months, I reached out to God, praying He'd forgive me for the choices I had made. I recognized my issues with alcohol and wanted to change. During a week-long revival at the church I attended, I was invited to speak on youth night to share my struggles with alcohol, drugs, and cigarettes. For some time after, I was committed to abstaining from these substances. I wanted to be the good church girl, and I was at times. Deep down, however, I wasn't ready to give up the lifestyle I had been living. Not long after, I found myself in the bars, in different relationships with no expectations. While I still tried to hide this life, feeling guilty, I continued searching for someone to love me and to fill the void within me.

I went off to an all-women's college. Again I tried to redefine myself. My goal was to stay in control of my actions, to use proper etiquette, to appear to have it all together, and to have fun. I was given the opportunity to be an admission's representative, giving tours to prospective students. I was elected freshman class president. In the spring I pledged a sorority. I felt like I belonged. During this time, I met a baseball player in my music appreciation class. I started meeting him outside of class at his fraternity house for little visits. On one of these quick visits when he wasn't expecting me, I popped in just to say hi and found him smoking pot with some friends. I knew I would have to make a decision. I felt uncomfortable. My conscience was yelling at me, *What are you doing?* Although I wanted nothing to do with him, I let my guard down and started smoking pot with him and being with him.

As I struggled much that year with who I was, where I fit in, and with my morals and values—concerned about my reputation and how I was perceived—casual relationships like this one would continue and would involve many other people throughout the course of my life.

A few of the more substantial relationships would continue off and on, too. These relationships seemed to come and go for several years as we remained friends with a casual relationship on the side. Each time one of these guys came back into my life—each differently having a piece of my heart—I always wondered if that time was the time he would be coming back into my life for good.

The summer after my freshman year in college, I worked in Yellowstone National Park, and who showed back up? The guy who brought me the roses and balloons for my fifteenth birthday.

Later that night we sat at the top of Mammoth Hot Springs. It was pitch black. The sky was so clear that we could see all the constellations, the Milky Way, even the satellites going across the sky. It was magnificently beautiful. I couldn't believe that he was even here with me. As we sat next to each other on a ledge overlooking all of Mammoth Hot Springs, my legs dangling over the side, he pulls out a small square box and says, "I haven't been here for you for your birthday for the last four years."

Just being there with him made up for the past four years. I was so excited, and my heart was racing. What was in the box? As he handed it to me, I felt so special. I opened the box, and there was a diamond necklace. I must admit, of course, I wished it was a ring, but I had never received anything like this before. I hugged and kissed him. I was so thankful. I thought he had come back for me and was so in love with me. I wondered if this was really happening and what would happen next.

That week lasted for a blink of an eye, and off he was, out of my life, just as fast as he re-entered. Devastated and hurt once again, I picked up the pieces, went back to school for the fall semester, and continued to struggle.

During my junior year, I arrived back on campus for rush with my sorority. The son of a dear friend of my mom's had transferred to Westminster to be closer to his mom, who had cancer. One day when my mom was visiting her, he walked in and was introduced. My mom asked him, "Do you know my daughter, Susie?"

"Susie who?" he asked.

"Susie Jaramillo."

"Jaramillo?" he asked. "Susie Jaramillo? Yes, I know her." He had only been at school for a few weeks, but he had met me one night when I was out at Sir Winston's having appetizers and drinks with at least 20 of my sorority sisters. We were the life of the party, and he definitely remembered who we were after that night.

As soon as they realized we knew each other, they disappeared into the kitchen and quickly came up with a plan for him to visit me. Moments after that conversation, he showed up at my sorority house with a nicely packaged bunch of cookies. How sweet! Their plan worked, and we began dating.

The same issues came up in this relationship: sleeping together early on, drinking, and dealing with insecurities. While we spent many hours visiting with his mom and family, we spent most of our time at the bar to escape from much of what was going on in life. His mom was dying of cancer, and I was struggling with my life. The last night of the semester, I was studying, and he went out. The next morning after my final, I went over to his house and found him with someone else. I broke up with him immediately. I did not see this coming. Our families had been friends, and I had spent almost a year with him. I was hurt, angry, and devastated. And there went another piece of my heart.

Within weeks my girlfriend and I went down to the lake and met up with some of my sorority sisters at a local bar. After several beers, I did my usual, got up on the bar, got everyone's attention, and told a joke. A guy in the crowd caught my attention. Not too long after, he and his friends were talking with me and my friends, and we were introduced. He had just graduated from college and was a pilot. He showed interest immediately and was engaging. He called me within a few days, we met, went out, and soon began dating.

Not only did I find him attractive and find his career as a pilot exciting, he seemed to pay more attention to me and to openly show me affection. These actions drew me to him. I was willing to be at his beck and call. We lived an hour-and-a-half apart, and I would drive to visit him an average of once a week. At the end of that summer, he moved back to his hometown, which was five hours away. After that, I went back to school and we continued to see each other about once a month, sometimes every two weeks. We would drive hours to see each other and would take every opportunity to spend time together.

Because of the distance, we spoke often on the phone. This created a relationship where we relied on one another to tell each other the day's events and life experiences without seeing each other. While doing so, there were often times of miscommunication and accidentally hurting one another's feelings. While some of these situations would get resolved over the phone or the next time we met, some of them would go unresolved and would lead to a lack of trust. At the same time, it was so exciting to see each other face to face and enjoy one another's company. Once this excitement wore off, these issues would resurface.

After around 10 months of dating, I found myself pregnant. Wanting to do what we thought was the right thing at the time, we chose to have an abortion. From that point on, our relationship was never the same. The affection changed. The trust changed. The communication changed. I felt at that moment he didn't love me enough to have a baby with me. Although I never said anything to him, immediately I was angry inside at him for all I was having to go through mentally, physically, and emotionally. I wanted to blame him for it all, not wanting to look at myself and take responsibility, trying to mentally erase this experience, feeling so awful, and just wanting to hide. At the same time, I didn't want to lose him, was scared of being alone, and could already feel a separation happening between us. Once again I found myself in a vulnerable place.

Wanting to keep this relationship together, I searched for a job in the city where he lived, accepted one six weeks before graduation, packed a U-Haul three days after graduation, and moved to be close to him. What should have been a joyous occasion was not as big of an event as I was expecting. Instead of arriving to a welcoming party at my new apartment with balloons and a cooler, my girlfriend and I unloaded the truck by ourselves and headed to the nearest grocery store for our own celebration.

I was now away from home, lonely, and learned again to rely on myself. After being there some time, my boyfriend and I broke up. To fill the void of him in my life, I continued developing casual relationships with people I had just met, eventually giving some of them a piece of my heart. Some I would never see again, and others would become mere acquaintances in my life. Although I tried to move on, much sadness remained and I did all I could to get his attention again. Later that year, the boyfriend that I had moved to be with and I got back together. Several months later, I found myself pregnant again which led to another abortion. The distrust, hurt, and belief that he didn't love me were even more evident. Three months later he became physically abusive. We broke up.

I felt depressed, sad, and lost. We chose to end two lives. There was no changing those decisions we made. At the same time, I broke my hand, had four teeth pulled, totaled my car, got braces, and lost weight. Feeling overwhelmed but determined not to quit, I pushed for my next career move.

Within weeks, I received the approval to be transferred out of state with my job as an interior designer. I moved, started working on a new building, and met someone on site. I felt out of place, and he was someone I could spend time with. Within a short time, I felt smothered for the first time in my life. He was always there. I wasn't used to that; I did the chasing with most of the guys I was with up to this point.

Driven by my career, I received an opportunity to move to Dallas. Not feeling attached to this relationship, I accepted the transfer within my company and committed to being there in four weeks. During this time, I found out I was pregnant. As ashamed as I was of myself, I didn't want to be in a relationship where I felt restricted. I went to Dallas and had my third abortion. I didn't want any memory of who he was. I looked forward to what was ahead as a designer moving to a major city.

Dallas was different. Everything was big in the Lone Star State. Blonde hair, country bars, glass buildings, and the Dallas Cowboys were the highlights. Wanting to be more financially stable, I got a second job. The adage, "Time is money," always rang in my head. Pulling through the drive-through beer line one day and seeing how much fun our reggae friend was having hanging out the store window, I thought this might be something fun to do. After running inside and talking to the manager, I started work. My boss at my corporate job was not enthused at where I chose to work, but this job provided me a place to relax and have fun while making money. A few months later, I met someone through the drive-through beer line— dark hair, nice suit, and driving a BMW. The third time

I saw him, he asked for my number. He fit the image I had to be a yuppie couple together. We started dating. Having a seafood dinner in downtown Dallas with a glass of wine, I was falling for a romantic who was 10 years older than I was. Clearly he was looking for someone to settle down with. Unfortunately, my age, inexperience, insecurities, and issues with alcohol seemed to get in the way. After having a disagreement one night, we didn't speak for days. Hoping to resolve our differences, I decided to go see him. He opened the door, and someone else was in the background. He made it clear he could not speak to me and he was looking to get back together with his previous girlfriend.

Dishonesty and lack of trust seemed to be a theme in my relationship patterns. As much as I pointed the finger at each guy separately and how he hurt me, the reality was each could do the same to me. I asked myself continuously, *What do the words "I love you" truly mean? What is unconditional love? And what does that look like?* As each relationship ended, these were words I held on to. It seemed so simple: I wanted someone to love me and not leave me. Would I ever be the type of person someone would want to marry and spend the rest of his life with?

I worked 65 to 70 hours a week, and I still found time to have a social life. In the clubs in downtown

Dallas, the country bars and being twirled around on the dance floor by a cowboy (which I loved), out at the local pubs, or eating queso and drinking beer while watching a movie—I tried to enjoy life. While focusing on my career and having a social life, I had one rule: never date anyone you work with.

One morning, I woke up, looked around, and did not recognize where I was. I heard someone in the shower, and I panicked. I didn't know whose house I was in. I was in someone else's bed. Had we done anything? I looked at the clock and realized I was a couple hours late for work. Where was I, how did I get here, and where was my car? I had gone to our company Christmas party and decided to attend the after-party at a Dallas night club. My memory was blank after the point when, having had at least 10 beers and 6 or 7 shots, I had run up onto the stage, grabbed a tambourine, and started singing with the band. A guy I worked with walked into the room, ready to go to work, and asked me how I was. I couldn't believe who I was seeing. Embarrassed and feeling completely hung over, I smiled and acted as if it was no big deal.

He drove me to my car. He knew where it was; I didn't. As I drove back to my apartment, I couldn't get there, get ready, and get to work fast enough. I called my girlfriend in St. Louis to explain what I had done.

I assumed he and I had been together. From that night, we kept everything we did secret due to company policy. A few weeks later a group from work went out to one of the biggest country bars in Dallas. Well after midnight, with four of us still there, and several drinks later, we went home. He and I had secretly arranged earlier for him to follow me. The next morning, as he was leaving my place, he asked me for my number.

For five months, we saw each other and kept this relationship hidden. We didn't have the type of relationship where he would pick me up and go out on a date in public for fear of being seen by someone at work. When we did speak, I was often on my car phone and we would arrange to meet at his house. I became aware that he was separated from his wife for about six months and was currently going through a divorce. He made it sound as if it was no big deal, telling me he hadn't been married long. I didn't ask many questions.

Because of his area of expertise, he was offered a transfer to Miami to help jumpstart one of our division's newest stores. Within weeks, he accepted the position, the movers came and packed his things, and he moved to South Beach, Miami. Over the next seven months, we saw each other only three times— once in Miami soon after he moved, once in Atlanta for me to meet his family, and once in Missouri for him to meet mine. After finding out that our division was opening a new store in Fort Lauderdale, I put in for a transfer and was approved to be a designer. It was understood I would move in with him. Talk began of a long-term relationship.

Life was exciting again. I would be moving to South Beach—a vacation spot for Europeans, with yachts and cruise ships coming in and out of the Port of Miami from all over the world, the location of Star Island where many movie stars had homes, with movies often being filmed and magazine photo shoots with models taking place. My career would give me opportunities to work on a design team to build the interior of this new store, and would eventually lead to designing interiors for condominiums on the ocean and waterfront properties along the canals for a variety of people, including several millionaires. I moved in with him.

I learned from my grandmother that you were to be courted first. You dated and got to know each other. He would ask you to marry him. You would be engaged for a time and share your hopes and dreams. You would have a church wedding with your friends and family with punch and cake. You would go on a honeymoon where you would consummate your marriage, and then you would move in together upon your return. I had moved in with someone I wasn't married to. We had never attended church together and had never really talked about our religious beliefs. While his divorce would become final within a month, he was still married to someone else. This was not the order I was taught.

Upon my arrival, instead of enjoying the beach, I focused on getting everything in order and painting our place. One morning around three weeks after I moved in, while he was in the shower, I took a pregnancy test and it showed up positive. I knew I was; I knew that feeling. I contemplated what to say and do next. He didn't know I'd had three abortions previously. What would he say? What would we do?

"The test is positive, and I am pregnant. What do you want to do?"

From the shower, he paused and then answered, "Let's just get married and have the baby."

"Okay," I said.

I wasn't sure if I was ready to be married or to have a baby. I had dreamed of having my future husband, on one knee, saying, "I love you so much, and I cannot imagine spending the rest of my life without you. Will you marry me?" I imagined someone saying, "I can't wait to make a baby with you. You'll be so cute pregnant, and we'll have the cutest family." I never heard that. Waiting a few days to get the courage to tell my mom, we called our families and a few close friends and told them the news. What should have been the most exciting time in our lives—telling everyone we were getting married, that I was pregnant, and that we were going to have a baby—we hid from many of those around us, waiting to tell them we were pregnant until weeks after we got married.

Suddenly feeling scared, knowing I still struggled with drinking and boundaries, I wondered, *Could I be a good and faithful wife? Was I worthy to be pregnant? Would I be a good mother?* I kept telling myself, *I am keeping this baby.* Life had changed. Instincts kicked in.

We selected a destination wedding package through a resort in Negrile, Jamaica. The morning we got married, we rode in a glass-bottom boat and could see in the blue clear water many blue, yellow, and orange tropical fish. We snorkeled and enjoyed our morning together before getting married that afternoon. I left to have my hair done and prepare for our four o'clock ceremony, and he stayed on the beach. We sent drinks back and forth to each other. Fifteen minutes before our ceremony, I called my sister in the States to hear her sing to me over the phone a song I always dreamed she would sing from the balcony of a church at my wedding, *Ave Maria.* A resort assistant escorted me to the wedding ceremony. As people watched from their balconies, I walked down the aisle, which was actually a long sidewalk along the beach, to where he and the minister waited. He had fallen asleep at the beach, so—when I saw him in his white tux—he was sunburned and looking quite miserable. As we said our vows, the minister—who had verified the day before that I was a spinster and that my husband-to-be had been married before—gave me this look that seemed to ask, *Are you sure you want to do this?* I questioned myself, *Is this it? How did I get here?*

We had several visitors, which made for a stressful time while I was pregnant. As the temperatures rose quickly by March and April, I retained water and was nauseated the first several months. With my new husband's friends visiting, I woke up Mother's Day morning and he and his friends were nowhere to be found. This set the standard for what my life would be for the coming years. Lies, deceit, fighting, and arguing followed. At times we were able to mask these problems, but they never went away.

At 38 weeks into my pregnancy, a hurricane was projected to come through Miami. Our doctor recommended I go to the hospital because, when the barometric pressure drops, anyone 36 weeks pregnant or more could go into labor. After packing as many of our possessions as we could into two large bags, we waited until the last minute to go to the hospital. Because of the number of pregnant women who had arrived before us, no beds were left and we spent the night on the cold floor. The hurricane passed. No baby came.

A few weeks later, after gaining 60 pounds over the course of 9 months, I and my husband walked 18 blocks to help induce labor. Two days later, our son was born. That first night of our son's life, as the three of us slept in my hospital bed, I never knew how much love and joy I would instantly feel for this child. Because I had allowed myself to love him while I was carrying him during my pregnancy, I had formed a bond with him. I was thankful for his life.

For the next 10 months, we enjoyed watching our son grow, took numerous walks, and rollerbladed or ran behind his jogger stroller. Often on Friday nights, we would take a cab to have dinner at restaurant called the Big Pink, have several drinks, and enjoy the culture and nightlife along Collins Avenue.

In the spring of that next year, my husband received the opportunity to be transferred back to his hometown in the Atlanta suburbs. While moving from the beach to the suburbs would be a huge culture shock, we decided that this location closer to his family would be a better place for us to raise children. We moved into a lovely home with all the amenities in a swim-tennis community.

Stresses came with this move that I had not anticipated. I did not have a close relationship with his mother. I didn't love her as my own mother, and I didn't feel as if she loved me as her own daughter. I often felt uncomfortable. I learned to never get between a mother and her son.

He allowed other people to influence him. Whether with old friends, new ones, or those he worked with, he started spending more time away from home, often late at night. This continued throughout our marriage. I hadn't met many people yet, I felt insecure with our relationship, and I constantly felt as if I was second to whomever lurked at every turn. When he was home, he often helped with our son so I could paint our house or get other projects done. While his mom would occasionally watch our son so we could go out to dinner and work on projects together, we no longer had as much time together as a couple to catch up on the day's events, go for walks, and spend time as a family. I masked the hurt and pain, and made sure I kept my mouth shut to neighbors and anyone we worked with especially due to his job. I had been angry inside for so long, that I would let him have it at every opportunity when something did not go right. My tongue became my worst enemy. With this anger, I tore him apart with my words to hurt him as much as I felt hurt inside.

We found ourselves pregnant with our second child. We never discussed keeping the baby or not, so this was a new experience for me. I looked forward to being pregnant this time and enjoying these nine months. Our son was excited that he was going to be a big brother. We often read him books about being a big brother. He would get to experience the kicking and moving of his sibling in my belly.

The appointment arrived when we would find out the gender of our baby. As I lay there with my husband next to me, both anticipating the news, we were told, "It's a girl."

I began to cry, and that cry turned into weeping, to the point the person giving me the ultrasound asked, "Are you OK? Is everything alright?"

My life flashed before me. The decisions I had made seemed to meet me face to face. As I continued to cry, I said, "I don't want her to grow up and be like me." I wanted more for my little girl than I had given myself. I never explained the emotions I was feeling, and neither the staff nor my husband ever asked.

Preparing for her arrival was different because we lived in a house instead of an apartment on the beach. Originally I designed her room for simplicity with a light blue and yellow color scheme. One day I decided her room had to be pink and green with white bead board, complete with frilly dresses and bows for her hair. As her dad worked hard to install the bead board on all the walls, up to 60 inches high, her big brother, now 2, scrubbed her bathroom floor and vacuumed with his play vacuum, making sure everything was clean.

Although we attended church in Florida after our son was born, we stopped going after we moved to Atlanta. At this time we agreed it was important to attend church as a family. We visited several churches, and—while I was pregnant—we found our church home. From then on, we attended a Sunday school class for married couples, and our children became involved in the children's ministry during the next several years.

Several months before our daughter was born, my husband received a promotion to be at the corporate office for the company we worked for. This was exciting news. He would have the opportunity to work and travel across the country, would receive a financial increase, and would work closely with the decision makers in his department. Although this promotion was a good career move, it put a strain on me as I was pregnant and taking care of our son while working full time.

Three weeks before our daughter's due date, we were told that something wasn't right with my pregnancy. They ordered an ultrasound and found out that our daughter was breech; instead of her head being down, her legs and head were up. We were told that due to the fluid pockets surrounding her, she was a candidate to be turned on the outside of my womb. We scheduled this appointment and were told to be prepared; due to the pressure upon her, I might have to go into an emergency C-section. We arrived for the appointment, and two doctors began the process of trying to turn her around. I looked down, saw her body sideways, and said, "Please keep trying to push her. I do not want a C-section." As painful as it was, after 30 minutes, they stopped. I begged them to do it one more time. As they began to get her to the halfway point, she wasn't willing to turn the rest of the way. We scheduled the C-section.

Within days our daughter was born. She was beautiful. During a three-hour period when she and I remained in post-op due to some of her levels, I bonded with her. While I was nervous, not fully understanding her condition, I remained calm and continued to feed her to help increase these levels. This was a sweet, gentle, and quiet time for us. After his family went home, the four of us spent time together, uninterrupted, and our son was able to hold his baby sister.

When she was eight weeks old, my daughter, son, and I flew to my hometown for my family and friends to meet her. My husband remained behind for work. For the next week I enjoyed seeing my mom, my grandmother, my sister and her family, and friends. This was an exciting time for us. Over the weekend and into the next week, upon our return to Atlanta, I learned that my husband made decisions while we were apart that would affect the rest of our marriage. After learning more of the truth, my anger raged to the point I put my fist through a sidelight window at our front door.

Within months we attended a marriage retreat with a few hundred people at a local church. The retreat began on a Friday evening and went through Saturday afternoon. We attended the first evening together, and much wisdom was poured into us. At times I felt convicted of the many mistakes I had made as a wife in disrespecting my husband. I remember 1 Corinthians 13 being read, "Love is patient, love is kind. It does not envy, it does not boast, it is not proud. It is not rude, it is not self-seeking, it is not easily angered, it keeps no records of wrongs. Love does not delight in evil, but rejoices with the truth. It always protects, always trusts, always hopes, always perseveres. Love never fails.... And now these three remain: faith, hope and love, but the greatest of these is love."

Wow, is all I could think. I had failed. How could I take back all the hurtful words I had said to demean him and hurt him? How had we gotten to this place of such devastation in our marriage? I had not been as loving and supportive as God calls a wife to be. How do you forgive not only yourself for causing such hurt but forgive the one who has hurt you the most? There wasn't a magical formula to fix where we were, or was there? We seemed to want to keep our marriage together but didn't know how to remove the anger and bitterness and division we were dealing with. The exact opposite happened, and we got into a fight during the seminar and did not sit with each other for much of the day. I got up before that session was over and went to the prayer room. In tears I poured out to a prayer couple some of the troubles in our marriage. I pointed the finger at him and did not own my weaknesses.

It was evident to both of us that we needed help. We started meeting with a local Christian couple who did marriage counseling together. We met with them several times, sometimes going as a couple and sometimes individually. After skimming the surface of our marriage relationship, we didn't hold ourselves accountable to work on the issues we had. While my husband wanted to focus on the future of our relationship, I was too busy looking at the past. We had reached a point in our relationship that, when he spoke, I could no longer decipher the truth from a lie. After seeing them for less than three months, we never returned.

After our daughter was around six months old, I received a promotion as a designer to travel throughout the country. I loved what I was doing. With both of us traveling regularly for our careers, I traveled during the first part of the week when he was home and he traveled during the second part of the week when I was home. While I was being careful not to put myself in inappropriate situations, I noticed he began to miss Friday flights home. Traveling, parenting two young children, and feeling more like roommates than a married couple, we again sought counseling.

We saw an individual counselor. At first, she counseled us together. Then she met with us individually, occasionally bringing us together. Once again, my husband wanted to focus on the future; I needed to find resolution from our past and present.

One night we were in the kitchen arguing. Our four-year-old son tugged on my leg and said, "Mommy, please stop fighting." I knew I did not want our children to learn love looked like this.

After separating twice, I went outside our marriage to find fulfillment. While I had been faithful to this point, I broke our vows. After a year-and-a-half of counseling, separating now for the third time, I filed for divorce.

Six months later we tried one more time to save our marriage. A woman from our Sunday school class asked me to read the book, *When Godly People Do Ungodly Things*. I realized I needed to ask my husband's forgiveness in several areas. Inviting us to dinner, this woman and her husband tried to help us reconcile. Later that evening, as my husband and I were in their living room by ourselves, and they, upstairs, praying, I knelt and my eyes filled with tears. I apologized for my shortcomings and my anger, and also confessed what I had done outside of our marriage. Although I felt vulnerable for telling the truth, it felt good. I hoped he too would reveal much that had been hidden. Nothing was revealed.

So much did not come to the surface. Hurt, anger, and resentment remained in my heart. We pointed our fingers at one another for dysfunctions and couldn't get on the same page. With the lies, the alcohol, my screaming and yelling, and the constant blaming, things seemed desperate. With my being fatherless and his father being absent during some of his childhood, neither of us knew what a healthy relationship looked like. We had lost trust and didn't know how to get that back. Why did things seem to be so complicated?

We felt no attraction toward one another. Things I desired—sweet kisses here and there, and physical touch—we didn't share. We were two married people, living two separate lives. Our marriage ended after six-and-a-half years. That time was the loneliest and saddest time of my life. Feeling lost like never before, I was so broken you could have scraped me off the floor.

I continued searching for love. A dear friend encouraged me to sign up with an online dating service. I met several people in different states. Distance became a challenge. I protected my children and did not involve them in these relationships. I did meet someone who shared similar interests—running, cycling, camping, and other outdoor activities. We dated on and off for over a year. He was so kind and gentle, and we enjoyed one another's company.

Unfortunately, something was missing. Although we both attended church and shared the same faith, with no mention of marriage, I gave myself to him. We both had trust issues and hurt still remained from past relationships.

I didn't respect myself enough to stand my ground on the values I was taught as a child. I didn't love unconditionally; with every relationship, there was a condition. Would I ever be able to love someone unconditionally, and would I be able to receive love?

TWELVE

THE POWER OF PRAYER – SOUL TIES BROKEN

"Flee from sexual immorality. All other sins a person commits are outside the body, but whoever sins sexually, sins against their own body. Do you not know that your bodies are temples of the Holy Spirit, who is in you, whom you have received from God? You are not your own; you were bought at a price. Therefore honor God with your bodies."
— *1 Corinthians 6:18-20*

After Amy commanded all soul ties that were not of God to come out, she said, "Name the men you have been with, saying their names one by one, and then ask that those you cannot remember be included, that all soul ties with these guys be broken." I did.

Amy said, "I take authority over and I bind all soul ties that are not of God, and I command you to release her in the name of Jesus." As she continued to pray, this spirit loosened its grip, and I began throwing it up. The release was long and steady. Because the release was so strong, I held onto Amy's forearm. Once it was fully released, I gasped for air, finally able to breathe again.

Amy continued, "Lord God, I ask that You go get all of the emotional and spiritual pieces of her heart that she has given out to all these people and that are still in their grip, and we ask that You bring them all back together and make her whole in You, in the name of Jesus."

All parts of my being, strewn everywhere with everyone, were being restored to me for my wholeness. My heart—which I had given so many times, and which had been dropped and shattered into pieces—He was rewriting.

Something bigger and greater than humanity had to first find the pieces of my heart and then start to put them back in place. With the complete release of this spirit, the breaking of all the soul ties, and my heart being made whole in a way that I could have never imagined, all the hurt, lies, bitterness, and feelings of being unworthy to be loved were removed. I found out the power of God through strategic, anointed, Holy Spirit prayer.

He released me from all of this spirit's involvement that I had yielded to for so long. Searching for love, I had given my heart while trying to find that person to fill the void in my life. In all these relationships, I searched for a love that no guy could ever give me. This love that I had been searching for could only come from God, and I received it that day. I would learn His love as a Father, as a Husband, and in return I would now be able to love and be loved.

Remaining in a place of complete submission to the power of the Holy Spirit, we continued.

She said, "Spirit of control, I call forth all manipulation, seduction, lies, and control. You have been found out, and it's time to go in the name of Jesus!"

THIRTEEN

CONTROLLING SPIRIT

*"Like a city whose walls are broken through
is a person who lacks self-control."*
— *Proverbs 25:28*

"Where is your dad?" a kid from my third-grade class asked. He had always seen my mom drop me off, had never seen my dad, and had never heard me talk about him.

"He doesn't live here," I said, not knowing the truth, not wanting to lie, and hoping to avoid the question. This was not a topic I talked about.

"So where is he?" he continued.

Now what do I say? I thought. "He lives in Spain," I heard myself say.

I felt out of control because of the secret that seemed to linger: who was my father? I felt out of control due to the situations that surrounded me. Not knowing my identity, my life became a game of covering up, hiding, and ignoring reality. When I asked my mom who my dad was, she wouldn't tell me. Why was it such a secret? I often thought this inner torment of not knowing the truth began that day when I was four when my sister told me I was adopted, but I also wondered if it started earlier. Isn't one of a baby's first words *Dada*? Or did it start even earlier when I was in my mother's womb?

In my family—through spoken and unspoken expectations—I was brought up to act and dress appropriately, to have composure, to use manners, and to present myself well, no matter where I was or who I was with, especially when in public. I was concerned about how I was perceived, and I always felt as if people were judging me.

I had no control over knowing who my father was, over the finances in my home, and over my brain's ability to comprehend books I read in school and stories I heard in church. I wanted to control my destiny. I wanted to be successful.

I tried to control situations in grade school such as four square and kickball, softball, and basketball at school. I was athletic and very competitive. I realized even at that young age that being on a team didn't always mean you had people on the team who were equally competitive and athletic. If the objective was to win, why wasn't everyone on the same page? When someone didn't make a play or wasn't performing at the level I thought they should, I would raise my voice at them. I coached them by telling them what to do, but often I would end up hurting their feelings.

While playing soccer during gym class in eighth grade, I shouted instructions to teammates and at one point got upset with one of the girls for making a mistake. My gym teacher, who was also a high-school girls track coach that commanded respect, said, "Susan, go up to the locker room and get changed. I will be up there to talk to you."

She was one I didn't want to mess with. I was also mad at myself, mad because I had hurt someone else's feelings through what I said and how I said it. All I wanted was to be liked and accepted. A verse came into my head often when things like this would happen, "Treat others as you would like to be treated." I didn't do that.

When she arrived, she sat next to me and said, "Susan, you are a leader, and many are looking up to you. You cannot yell at people. That's not how you treat others. No matter how frustrated you get or what you think they should be doing, you do not speak to them in that manner."

I didn't realize what this coach was actually trying to speak into my life about being a leader and how important delivery was when you communicate. All I could think about was how disappointed she was in me, how disappointed I was in myself, and how I hoped no one was mad at me from my class. I didn't hear recognition for how good I was on the field. That day and many other times, others tried to speak into my life and all I heard was the negative. I didn't know how to take constructive criticism.

Midway through junior high I chose to focus on my running. One hot summer day our team was practicing for some time, and we were tired. After our coach instructed us what to do next, I got upset and yelled, "I quit!"

Getting in my face, he said, "I don't ever want to hear you say that again." I got in line and did what he said. I never made that statement again—even when I was tired, didn't believe in myself, and wanted to quit.

He reinforced what my mom always taught: You never quit what you start, and you persevere until the end. This discipline and motivation stayed with me throughout track and cross-country, including a trip to State, and through the running I continued in my adult life. I learned to rely on my discipline and my motivation to achieve success in my life.

I didn't want to be called out, and I didn't want anyone holding me accountable for my actions. I didn't do well with confrontation. My automatic response was defense. In grade school I began noticing the dynamics in relationships. I had no idea that these cliques would be a social norm going forward. Often, I found my feelings hurt by those who ganged up on me, yet I must admit I did the same to others. I learned to maneuver in and out of social groups. This allowed me to have fun and enjoy having different friends in a way I felt safe. I was cautious how close I got to others. I seldom had to deal with the drama of group dynamics; usually the only drama I dealt with was my own.

Although I was strong-willed and independent, when it came to relationships with guys, the manipulation of myself and others began. I lied to hide my insecurities and the truth of who I was, hoping someone would like me. I never felt as if I was able to be myself. They might learn something about me they didn't like, and that would give them a reason not to be with me. What I didn't realize was that many guys were also looking for validation.

I thought love looked like attention and intimacy. As a result, I would get into romantic situations, both with guys I knew and with complete strangers. Although I would say I was in control, I was out of control. Often I would have a few drinks—"liquid courage," I called it—to boost my confidence before I went out. Hiding the real me, at times I would seduce, manipulate, and give a piece of myself to whomever I might encounter. I was not aware of the degree to which they were manipulating me, too.

One night in a relationship that spanned several years with someone I thought I knew, I found myself in a situation I could have never imagined. Having waited several hours on a night I was expecting him to visit, I went to bed. Upon his arrival after two in the morning, he wanted to be with me. Having learned how to control guys by withholding myself from them and angry that he had stayed out so late drinking with a group he worked with, I resisted his advances. He began to threaten me verbally. Within seconds he straddled me in bed, holding my arms down with his knees, and began to strangle me with his right hand. His strength was more than I could handle, and this deep anger seemed to well up within him. I screamed several times, "Please, please don't kill me," and I begged God, *Please let me live*. A strength I cannot explain allowed me to free my arm and hit him on the back of his head with my fist turned in a way that didn't even seem possible. He got off of me. Scared, crying, and not knowing what to do, I called the police.

As we waited for them to arrive, I sat in shock, not wanting to believe what had just happened and not wanting to do what I knew I had to do. I had never seen him this drunk or act like this before. At that moment, I knew in the core of who I was that if a relationship became abusive, I had to get out. It was time for the mental, verbal, and physical abuse to stop. This relationship was over. The police arrived. I chose not to press charges. He left. After going to the doctor the next day, I learned I had broken my hand on the back of his head.

After long-term relationships like this ended, I would find myself very lonely. Hurt, scared, confused, wondering what was next, how would I move on after all I'd been through, having trusted and relied on that relationship? After each one, I built the walls up higher and higher.

I focused on controlling my body, my environment, and my career. After coming out of serious relationships, I would not eat for days. I liked the change I noticed in my body and the compliments I received on how I looked. To regain control over myself, I would focus on being thin. Sometimes I would binge and purge, and I would often withhold myself from food. Some days I would only allow myself four crackers and some water or soda. Other times, I lived only on a baked potato for two meals a day. Some days I just didn't eat. I added exercise to the mix to get as lean as possible. The closer I got to what I considered a healthy weight, the more in control I felt.

Image was important to me. My smile was something I was always conscious of and embarrassed about. As soon as I got my own insurance, I got braces. I never smiled as big as I did when those braces came off. As a designer, conscious of how I dressed, I developed my own look—simplicity mixed with elegance and all *black*. Part of developing this image was learning how to speak and act. I knew when meeting someone for the first time, the first 10 seconds were the most important. I learned what a firm handshake was and why it was crucial to look the person in the eye.

I focused on making my environment as organized, presentable, and comfortable as possible. I learned over the years the cleaner and more organized my car, my work space, and my living space were, the more in control I felt. I redid almost every place I ever lived—fresh paint, flooring, fixtures, and occasionally additional furniture. I kept my car clean, washing and vacuuming it often. In my office environment, everything was filed in alphabetical order. Pens and paper clips were in containers. Keeping my environment organized, neat, and clean was a way to try to remain in control of what was going on around me. It helped mask the chaos in my life.

Since high school I lived by the adage, "Time is money." I always thought, *If I've got time, I might as well be making money.* Since reading Zig Ziglar's *See You at the Top*, I knew I didn't need to stay where I was.

I believed God was trying to get a hold of me through this book, giving me hope and showing me I could do anything. I did want more for my life, but I believed in worldly success. I thought success in my career would bring me happiness. It became both about titles and money.

Beginning with the work study program for Economic Development, Administrative Services, in high school, I learned proper business etiquette. Everyone there—the directors and their assistants—helped form the base of my business career. They encouraged me to set—and to live up to—high expectations. These expectations led me to having my first full-time job lined up 6 weeks before graduating from college and eventually to climbing the corporate ladder with several companies, including a Fortune 100 company.

My career allowed me to live in New York, Tulsa, Dallas, South Beach, and Atlanta. Achieving high-profile roles within some of these companies, I traveled both nationally and internationally, often weekly. My routine sometimes included day trips from Atlanta to New York to give a luncheon and then fly back. Designing for clients, including millionaires, I worked with some of the most prestigious companies throughout the United States. Through self-motivation, self-reliance, and perseverance, I positioned myself to make large salary increases. Within eight years I owned six different vehicles, including a brand-new Volvo, a couple of Land Rovers, and a Jaguar. My success allowed me to furnish my home with nice pieces, such as silk drapes, Oriental wool rugs, and decorative furniture. I was obtaining the worldly success that I had set out to achieve.

I appeared to be in control. I would be in beautiful, exotic places, on the beach, and should have been happy and content. I wasn't. On the inside, my heart and soul were crumbling. I was sad, lonely, and felt sorry for myself. Through my self-reliance, I had achieved so much; but at the same time, it wasn't enough to fill the empty and broken places in my life. I was trapped by addictions to smoking, drinking, and other drugs, which led me to make poor decisions that would affect my life. I was weighed down by the guilt and shame of taking the lives of three of my children through abortion to satisfy my needs and wants. I searched for answers through mediums, but never found what I was looking for. In spite of all I had achieved, I still lacked confidence in my ability to read and write. While I felt portions of love through my relationships with guys, I always placed false expectations on each relationship to give me the love that I was missing from a father and a love they would never be able to give me. I didn't feel worthy to be loved, I didn't love myself, and I wasn't able to love others fully. No amount of success—titles, status, money, and possessions—could fill the void within me. What was it going to take to mend my broken heart?

FOURTEEN

THE POWER OF PRAYER – SPIRIT OF CONTROL BROKEN

"But the fruit of the Spirit is love, joy, peace, patience, kindness, goodness, faithfulness, gentleness and self-control. Against such things there is no law. Those who belong to Christ Jesus have crucified the sinful nature with its passions and desires."
— Galatians 5:22-24

Continuing to be led by the Holy Spirit, Amy said, "Spirit of control, I command you and all manipulation, seduction, lies, and control to go in the name of Jesus! You have no dwelling place any longer and must leave in the name of Jesus!"

Still in this place of complete surrender to God's will, not knowing what was next but open and

141

trusting, I sank into my car seat, letting go of all the control over all those years. As this spirit was being drawn out, I could feel how vast this spirit's influence was in all areas of my life.

As this spirit was released, the walls I had put up came crumbling down. The rejection, hurt, pain, disappointment, lack of love, hatred for myself and others, anger, bitterness, resentment, brokenness, abandonment, loneliness, sadness, depression, and the lies were removed.

As I sat in amazement, I was now open to receive God's love and all He had for me.

FIFTEEN

THE POWER OF PRAYER –
SET FREE

*"'For I know the plans I have for you,' declares the
LORD, 'plans to prosper you and not to harm you, plans
to give you hope and a future. Then you will call on me
and come and pray to me, and I will listen to you. You
will seek me and find me when you seek me with all
your heart.'"*
— *Jeremiah 29:11-13*

We finally came to a place of full release and
surrender.

God had rewritten my heart, and I knew it.
Stillness had come over my car, and the warring was
over. The battling and fighting had come to a halt. We
were still and quiet. I took a deep breath, and took my
shirt and wiped my running nose as the tears fell. I
could feel a huge void within my very core. It actually

felt like the insides of me had been ripped, shredded, and stripped. There was the feeling of emptiness but unbelievable satisfaction. All my old tenants were gone. Thank God!

After getting my breath, I was grasping what had taken place. Amy began to pray for God to fill me with Him, with His abounding love, and to fill the very empty places with Himself. He put my heart back together in that prayer. I had prayed for forgiveness of all my sins. I had prayed that God would take over my life and restore my soul. I prayed that I would no longer rely on self but that He would lead and guide me all the days of my life. I thanked God for sending His Son Jesus, to die on that cross, that whosoever believes in Him should not perish but have everlasting life. I recalled at age 10 saying those very words of faith, yet this day I was making an adult dedication of my life, totally free of every enemy of the cross. I had asked that day that He fill me with His Holy Spirit so I could live my life the way He wanted me to.

Wow! A deep work of grace had taken place. I was fully aware and assured all my past had been removed, and His love now filled my heart. I was renewed to a place of innocence that I had lost at a young age. I was being given a second chance. He was the Lover of my soul and the One I would rely on from this day forth.

As we finished praying, I knew God loved me so much and that He arranged this divine appointment for me to be healed and delivered of the things that were destroying me.

From that moment on, I knew that I knew that I knew that God had changed my life and that I was now a woman of the Lord. I knew deep within me that I was to be respected as such. The relationship I was currently in, I knew I was not to be involved with anymore in the way that I had been. I was in a place of confidence that I knew who I was and I knew that I was God's.

As we began to say our good-byes for that day, Amy recommended that I take a nap. I laughed and smiled as she said that because I was exhausted. I felt like I had been through the ringer 50 times over, and at the same time I was in such a place of peace and stillness that I had never felt before. The life pain I lived with constantly was gone. The mental anguish was gone. The shame was gone. Although I could remember my past, I could not feel the shame, guilt, or pain any longer. I was changed and made whole in Him.

Within a few hours I called the guy I had been dating and told him I was a woman of the Lord now and I couldn't be with Him as I had been in the past. I knew I was not to share myself in that manner and I was to wait upon the Lord for the day when I was to be married.

Within the next day or two, Amy recommended I join a good Bible study with women. A study was starting up that next week at Mount Paran Church of God, called *Discerning the Voice of God* by Priscilla Shirer. I registered and began soaking in the Word of God. Week by week I began to discern the voice of God.

I had this constant desire to seek God and His love. I sought His face. I gleaned in His Word. I slept with my Bible on my heart, hoping God would download it into me. I read devotions daily. I listened to praise and worship music, and I would get into that place where it was just God and me. I learned to worship Him wherever I was and wherever I went, especially while I was running. I yearned to stay in this place with Him.

God's timing is perfect, and it's amazing how He orders our steps. God had changed my life. There was no denying that, and there was now a fire that was birthed deep within me that one eventful God day. There was no going back to the former life I had lived; I had been born again. God changed my life from the inside out.

SIXTEEN

SEVEN YEARS LATER –
WITH GOD, ALL THINGS ARE
POSSIBLE

*"And they overcame him because of the blood of the
Lamb and because of the word of their testimony...."*
— *Revelation 12:11*

Looking back on the seven years since that day Amy
prayed with me in my car, I would have never
imagined this journey God would lead me on. My life
was forever changed that day in January of 2007, and
I have never been the same since. I remain thankful for
God's sweet love for me and my children, the
mentoring I have received, the teachings, the
opportunities I have been given, and God's provision
for us along the way. I could have never imagined or

set out to do what God has placed before me. I have still had my share of struggles, but—through prayer, faith, hope, and the acceptance of wise counsel and correction of mentors—those times have provided such opportunities for growth.

Everything about me changed—my thinking, my focus, and the life that I had been accustomed to. I began to assess situations differently while learning healthy boundaries. Relationships changed, and some I let go of. My language changed. My thoughts and desires changed. Things I once found fulfilling and filled with purpose were no longer important. I saw the world in a whole new light. I began running after God, reading the Bible, participating in Bible studies, and attending workplace ministry conferences. I learned more about prophetic prayer, fasting, and healing. I attended church as much as I could, taking notes, learning Scripture, and gleaning from all I could get my hands on. I even began reading books on relationships, healthy boundaries, Biblical principles regarding finances, and God's giftings and purpose for our lives. How had I not heard anything about these areas before? A whole new world had opened up to me, and I could not get enough.

One area I never imagined conquering was addictions. Since the day I was prayed over, all desires for a drink, a cigarette, drugs, or anything else have been gone. God took away the struggles I could not overcome by myself; He overcame them with the blood of Jesus dying on the cross that bore my sins. For those of you struggling, do not take the bait of Satan, and do not let anyone talk you into having just one— one drink or one cigarette. It's a trap! Addiction can be overcome. Those around us do influence our decisions, and it is important to have healthy relationships and boundaries—these are a must! Ultimately, you make that decision. It was through stepping out in faith that God changed me and took those desires and removed them, but it has been up to me to continue to remain separated from that life that I once partook in. There is power in prayer, and—as I've experienced—I stand and believe that any stronghold can be broken, but we have to be willing to let it go.

With this newfound healthy lifestyle of not smoking and drinking, I found my lost love of athletics and nature. I began swimming, cycling, and running. Within the first two years, I participated in a biathlon, a triathlon, a mud/trail run, four half-marathons, and a full marathon in cities that included Atlanta, Georgia; Birmingham, Alabama; Burlington, Vermont; New York City, New York; and Dublin, Ireland. I was on fire, and there was no stopping me. Time spent running became a sweet time of prayer, listening to praise and worship music, and hearing God's still small voice. I cherish these times and hope to continue to train as long as the Lord allows me to.

In addition to healing me physically, God has taken me on a journey of healing, mentally and emotionally. Our lives are like an onion. God deals with us one layer at a time. God set me on a path of dealing with my past—past relationships, past hurts, and traumas—since my conception. While I had no plan of losing my job in 2009, it happened. The company closed. I lost everything I thought defined me—my job, my title, my six-figure income, and my house. God used that experience to ultimately lead me back to my hometown, a place I never imagined going back to, to do an inner work in me. Through the many challenges, I have learned not to look at circumstances but to trust God for His provision. He has gone before me to fight my battles and to make my path straight.

I learned the power of forgiveness. A few weeks before Christmas 2009, I was led to meet with my mentors, Ted and Sandy, to pray for some unforgiveness I could feel on my heart—for my mom and her never telling me the truth about my father, and for my children's father for the continued court battles over the past several years. A few weeks later I had gotten into my car to go to the Social Security office due to me thinking I had misplaced the kid's Social Security cards. I felt the prompting of the Holy Spirit to go back in my house and to fill out a form for myself. Not wanting to, I got out of the car and stomped back in the house, saying "Fine! Alright already." I filled out the form, got back in the car, and drove on. As I gave the form to the lady behind the window, she verified my mother's information and then verified what I never imagined I would hear: my father's information. As I cried on the other side of that window and she looked at me, I thanked her for giving me the information that would forever change my life. Not knowing what was happening with me, she sat amazed and didn't know what to say or do. I immediately texted Amy and told her what was happening, and then texted a friend who did intelligence work to see if she could find out where he was. Come to find out, he was only 40 minutes away. My heart raced, and my curiosity grew. Thirty-eight years had passed, and here I was at a moment of truth. God answered my prayer, revealing the truth of my earthly identity.

Within 48 hours of receiving the information, I contacted him, met him, and asked if he knew my mother. After a brief conversation about how he knew her and him asking me why I was there, he said, "I'm sorry, but I can't help you." Emotionally exhausted, within a few hours I reached out to my mom, shared with her all that had happened the last few days, and learned the truth—"That man raped me." I learned all that my mom endured and how she protected me, from the day I was conceived to the day she finally gave birth to me, making the decision to keep me. I was her baby, and she loved me despite the circumstances. I learned that day the love of a mother and how my life was spared.

This revelation led to further healing about a year later. While visiting the director of a pregnancy resource center to learn more about their organization, I was asked to share my story with a training class. Following that experience, I was introduced to several key people over the next 21 days that God would use to reveal the direction that He would lead. Doors began to open. At a pregnancy center banquet in Rolla, I heard Melissa Ohden speak about surviving an abortion. I bawled my eyes out. I knew what God was calling me to do—to tell my story. Afterwards, I introduced myself and shared my past. She recommended I take a post-abortive healing class. I was then introduced Carl Landwehr, President of the Vitae Caring Foundation. After sharing life experiences during our first meeting, he said, "Susan, you have a story to tell." God was confirming the direction I was to walk. That same week I was given the opportunity to attend a conference at the Lake of the Ozarks. God led me directly to Lori Driggs, Executive Director of If Not for Grace Ministries, an abortion recovery program. I signed up that day for the healing study—*Her Choice to Heal*, by Sydna Masse. This study took me to the depth that I had avoided and covered up for years. While already having been forgiven by God, I forgave myself and the others who were involved. This experience led me to start a post-abortive healing ministry. The following week, I met Kathy Forck, the Director of a local 40 Days for Life, while praying in front of an abortion clinic. After we talked, she invited me to speak at their upcoming banquet. I was blown away by the connections and appointments that God had set before me.

Before I went any further sharing my story publicly, I received wise counsel encouraging me to share with my family the truth about my past. I did. Sitting on my daughter's bed, I said to my children, "There's something I need to tell you...."

Already aware of differences in our family's life since that day when God rewrote my heart, Cameron said, "Wow, Mommy, God really did change you."

Separately, I shared with my mother all of my past. She looked at me and said with tears in her eyes, "I'm so thankful you made it through everything." I did—only by God's grace.

Right when I was getting ready to start speaking, I recall a close friend asking, "Are you sure you want to share these things about your life?"

I replied, "I feel led to. God is calling me to share the truth about my experience to help set others free."

As God led, I began speaking my story as opportunities presented themselves. After I spoke at a pregnancy center fundraising event at Texas A&M, Ugandan Minister Isaac Mukisa introduced himself and said, "You must come to my country and speak to my people."

Immediately I said, "Yes," with my arms raised, and then I said, "Wait. We must pray about this first." Over the next few months, Isaac and his wife Annabelle Skyped with me, and we continued to pray for God's will in our meetings together. In June of 2013 a team was formed, and I traveled to Uganda to partner with them. Sharing the message of the Gospel, we ministered to those hurting from so many situations involving alcohol, drugs, abandonment, abuse, rape, incest, abortion, and murder. A new ministry—The Remnant Generation—was birthed.

God has continued opening doors for me to work with many amazing organizations across the United States and in other countries. No matter where I am called to speak—churches, schools, universities, state capitols, conferences, fundraising banquets, television and radio programs, and prisons—I am thankful to see God setting others free. God loves us so much and wants to release us from anything that would separate us from Him. There is no limit to what God can do in our lives if we are willing to surrender to Him.

After that day when Amy prayed with me, my thinking about relationships changed and I was learning to guard my heart. While God took away my desire for drinking and smoking, God did not take away my desire to love and be loved. God had to teach me His love as a Father and as a Husband. I have had to learn many lessons about appropriate boundaries, living in reality and not fantasy, avoiding red flags, and accepting that I cannot make someone love me—all while "having my hand slapped" a few times along the way. I realized that just because my boundaries had changed, that did not mean the people around me would agree with—or respect—those boundaries. After experiencing heartache when trying to make a few relationships work, I finally got to the point where I had to let go, walk in faith, and trust that God had a plan for my life and anyone He might be preparing for me.

I have also learned to set boundaries in the areas of sorcery and witchcraft. Certain TV shows and movies, tarot card readers, Ouija boards, and horoscopes—I don't go there anymore. While some are still searching for answers from fortunetellers, I stand close to the Word on this subject and I've learned to rely on the direction and the revelation of the Holy Spirit. We do live in a spiritual world, and we are in a spiritual battle daily.

I know God has a plan and purpose for each of us, and I've learned that I have to step out of the boat, walk in faith, and trust in the direction God leads me. After I was led back to my hometown, the job I had been promised disappeared. One day at the dentist's office, God used a person's nametag to prompt me to apply for an MBA. I could hear people saying, "How are you going to afford this? You're a single mom. You don't have a job? There's no way possible." Within an hour, I was signing up for graduate school and checking with my mom to see if she could watch the kids every Monday for eighteen months. Classes began that next Monday.

Six months later, a couple who were missionaries serving in another country spoke at my church. As I heard them tell their stories, my heart cried out and prompted me to speak with them after the service. Sharing with them how God had changed my life through prayer, I said, "I'm praying for an evangelistic husband."

"Sweetie," she said, "what are you waiting for? You are the evangelist."

I answered, "I'm not an evangelist. I'm a corporate businesswoman, and as soon as I'm done with my MBA I'm headed back into corporate America."

Within a few weeks I felt prompted to send a list of seminaries to my mentors and two others, and asked them to pray for God's direction. One of the people receiving my list, my childhood church choir director, reached out to me and set up an appointment for me to meet the president of Central Baptist Theological Seminary. At the end of a two-hour meeting with the president during which I shared my heart, the president said, "I would like to offer you a full ride to get your Master of Divinity."

Prior to the day God changed me, I struggled with education. I was now being offered the opportunity to begin a second master's program. I had not completed the first one in my hometown yet, and I had no idea how I would now be able to drive to Kansas for the second one 3 hours away, afford gas, and have a place to stay while attending classes there a few days a week. I prayed. I trusted. God directed. God provided.

Once receiving the scholarship, I called my mother and told her all that had happened. As I cried, she was excited for me. She agreed to stay with the kids while I was away and agreed we'd make it work. After praying with my pastor and asking God for provision, I received a Second Chance Scholarship from Zonta, an organization that supports local women in the community. I received an additional scholarship from Park Avenue Baptist Church in Eldorado, KS, to participate in a medical mission to Nicaragua to provide water purification systems.

I walked in obedience to what I was called to do. I completed my Master of Business Administration in 2011. I completed my class work for seminary in May of 2013. Before graduating with my Master of Divinity in 2014, I took another leap of faith. I applied for the Doctor of Ministry program at Regent University and prayed once again for financial favor. God once again granted the financial means for me to begin my doctoral studies; I received two additional scholarships. Unbelievable!

Seven years ago, I was in such a dark place, feeling trapped by the enemy, with no place to turn. *What was a prayer going to do?* I had asked. For me, that prayer changed my life forever. I surrendered to God's will. I learned to trust His daily provision. I received God's grace, mercy, forgiveness, and love; and I was led to forgive others and myself. I learned to recognize Satan's snares.

I continue to pray for God's will for my life, and the plans and purposes He has for me.

"Our Father which art in heaven,
Hallowed be thy name. Thy kingdom come,
Thy will be done in earth, as it is in heaven.
Give us this day our daily bread.
And forgive us our debts, as we forgive our debtors.
And lead us not into temptation,
but deliver us from evil:
For Thine is the kingdom, and the power, and the glory,
for ever. Amen."
— Matthew 6:9-13(KJV)

EPILOGUE

Experiencing transformation before my very eyes is the most rewarding aspect of a life of investment and involvement with another. Susan is a rare jewel.

Investing in Susan has been such a rewarding gift. She is one who is passionate and focused in the new life God gifted her to walk out. As the reader revisits Susan's life journey and stories, know that the brief synopsis contained in these pages only touches the highlights of the depth of this young woman's ability to press toward all God opens to her.

Rarely does a mentor find one so dedicated and thankful to be freed, that she's fully on board before direction is given. She's the race horse, at the gate, ready for the sound of the bell and the gate to be lifted...to run the race before her in excellence, dedication, and discipline...whatever it takes.

Susan has made up her mind; she wants to please the One Who called her. She wants to accomplish all set before her in excellence. There's never a 'No' when the Lord says 'Go' to Susan.

You'll be handing this book to many.

>An inspiration.
>An example.
>A forward nudge to the hesitant.
>Encouragement to those limping along in life with a similar story.
>An enthusiastic no-excuses read for those who want to pursue new life despite personal hurdles.

Susan inspires us all.

May her story release renewed faith in a powerful God Who still changes lives.

Amy

NOTES

Chapter 1: Tired of Hiding Behind a Mask
      1.   Psalm 51:10-12 NIV

Chapter 2: The Power of Prayer
      1.   James 4:7 NIV
      2.   Romans 10:9 NIV

Chapter 3: The Seduction of Addictions
      1.   2 Corinthians 10:3, 4 NIV

Chapter 4: The Power of Prayer –
   Spirit of Addictions Broken
      1.   Mark 11:24 NIV

Chapter 5: The Lies of Abortion
      1.   Jeremiah 31:15 NIV

Chapter 6: The Power of Prayer –
   Spirit of Abortion Broken
      1.   1 John 1:9 NIV

Chapter 7: Witchcraft
      1.   2 Thessalonians 2:9 NIV

Chapter 16: Seven Years Later –
    With God, All Things Are Possible
1. Revelation 12:11 NASB
2. Matthew 6:9-13 KJV

FOR MORE INFORMATION

ON SUSAN'S STORY,

AND THE LATEST NEWS

AND EVENTS,

VISIT HER ON THE WEB AT

WWW.SUSANJARAMILLO.COM

CPSIA information can be obtained
at www.ICGtesting.com
Printed in the USA
FFOW03n1530160118
44456433-44248FF